D1452026

A PRAYER BOOK
FOR ORTHODOX CHRISTIANS

A
PRAYER BOOK
FOR ORTHODOX
CHRISTIANS

TRANSLATED FROM THE GREEK BY THE

HOLY TRANSFIGURATION
MONASTERY

BOSTON, MASSACHUSETTS
2009

Copyright © 1987 by the
Holy Transfiguration Monastery
Brookline, Massachusetts 02445
All rights reserved • Printed in Canada
Fifth Printing, Second Edition 2009
ISBN 0–943405–01–7
Library of Congress catalogue card number 87–82719

CONTENTS

THE PRAYER IN THE GARDEN

✝

PRAYER is the time of standing at the gate of the King to make supplication; and the entreaty of him that beseeches and makes supplication is fittingly granted at this time. Indeed, what other time is there when a man is so ready and carefully watchful as at the very time of prayer?

Saint Isaac, *Homily 23*

✝

PREFACE

In the Name of the Father, and of the Son,
and of the Holy Spirit. Amen.

> Watch and pray, that ye
> enter not into temptation.
> MATTHEW 26:41

OUR Lord and Saviour, by both word and example, has taught us and enjoined us to pray. To the prophet Esaias, He revealed in vision the Thrice-holy Hymn of the six-winged Seraphim; to the shepherds who kept watch by night, He revealed the angelic doxology; and to the disciples who in humility acknowledged that they did not know how to pray and besought Him, "Lord, teach us to pray, as John also taught his disciples," He opened His blessed mouth and surrendered to us that holy prayer, the "Our Father."

Thus, it is from our Lord and God Himself that we have received the beginning of the holy collection of prayers which have been bequeathed to us by Prophets, Apostles, and God-bearing Fathers inspired by the Holy Spirit.

These prayers form an incomparable treasury

and companion for Christians. By using these sacred prayers of the righteous of every age, we are guided and instructed in true contrition, in supplication, and in the adoration and glorification which are due to God. How many generations of Christians have been blessed and sanctified using these very prayers! Indeed, how many believers, though often unlearned and living amidst poverty, afflictions, and persecutions, have committed many of these prayers to memory and recalled them throughout the day and night!

In the Psalms we encounter the verse, "Seven times a day have I praised Thee for the judgments of Thy righteousness" (Psalm 118:164), and the Church in her wisdom offers us seven occasions throughout the night and day to praise the Creator with "psalms and hymns and spiritual songs" in the services of the Midnight Prayers and Matins, the Hours, Vespers, and Compline. These services are found in the *Horologion* (the *Book of Hours*), and from this we have compiled and translated the Morning Prayers, the Prayers at Mealtime, and the Services of Small Compline, Vespers, and Matins.

All of the audible parts of the Divine Liturgy of Saint John Chrysostom have been included. The Divine Liturgy of Saint Basil the Great differs from this in only four places. These also have been added to this text to allow for its use in both Divine Liturgies.

From the cycle of hymns of the week and of the liturgical year we have provided selected hymns chanted on Sundays and weekdays, as well as hymns from the principal feasts, the *Triodion*, and the *Pentecostarion*. Following the example of a Greek *Prayer Book* printed some two centuries ago in Venice, we have included the Service of Paschal Matins with the Paschal Canon. It would be of great benefit to Orthodox Christians to use this Canon every Sunday, since the Resurrection of our Saviour is celebrated on this day. Our holy Father Seraphim of Sarov chanted it throughout the year. He was heard chanting it on the eve of his blessed repose, which was in the night toward the morning of the second of January, in the year 1833.

The *Prayer Book* also includes The Akathist Hymn to our Sweetest Lord Jesus Christ, and The Akathist Hymn to the Most Holy Theotokos. This latter work is one of the most profound and beautiful compositions which we have received from Byzantium's sacred hymnographers, bearing eloquent witness to the Orthodox Church's belief in the mystery of the Incarnation of the Son of God, and devotion to the "Virgin who conceived and bore a Son."

We have given in their entirety the Supplicatory Canon to our Lord Jesus Christ, both the Small and Great Supplicatory Canons to the Most Holy Theotokos, and the Supplicatory Canon to the Guardian Angel of a Man's Life. All of these are meet "in every calamity and affliction of soul."

The last section of the *Prayer Book* contains The Service of Preparation for Holy Communion, and the Thanksgiving prayers to be read after Holy Communion.

All of the prayers and hymns in this *Prayer Book* have been translated by the monastery from the Greek texts. Four of the canons – the Small and Great Supplicatory Canons to the Most Holy Theotokos and the Supplicatory Canons to our Lord Jesus Christ and to the Guardian Angel – have been set to the metre of the hymns in the original Greek; however, all of the hymns and troparia can be executed in the original, liturgical chant of the Church.

The Services of Vespers, Matins, and the Small and Great Supplicatory Canons to the Most Holy Theotokos have been included in the *Prayer Book* in a format which would allow for their use in church. These services may also be said privately, or used in church when there is no priest, with these differences:

Begin all services with the exclamation, "Through the prayers of our holy Fathers, Lord Jesus Christ our God, have mercy on us. Amen," and continue with the introductory prayers as set forth for a reader.

In place of the longer litanies of the deacon, "Lord, have mercy," is said twelve times. In place of the Small Litany of the deacon, "Lord, have mercy," is said three times. All the exclamations of the priest are omitted.

The Gospels are read in an ordinary voice.

All other psalms, hymns, and prayers are read or chanted as when a priest serves.

Conclude all services with the exclamation, "Through the prayers of our holy Fathers, Lord Jesus Christ our God, have mercy on us. Amen."

The Apostle of the Nations enjoins us to "pray without ceasing," and this goal of uninterrupted noetic prayer remains the goal of every Christian. In our times, however, we are faced with demands and distractions which make this goal all the more difficult. We would therefore especially urge all Christians to spend time in prayer in the morning, to remember the prayers before and after meals, and to read the Service of Small Compline in the evening. Every day, monastics are enjoined to read the Akathist to the Theotokos as part of their daily rule of prayer, and we would also commend this practice to all Orthodox Christians. These are small things, and yet the establishment of them as a cycle of daily prayers is of very great importance to our spiritual life:

> In the spirit of revelation these small things have been laid down to be accomplished in our cells for the preservation of our life by wise men who uphold the institutes of the Church, but the unwise consider their omission as of no consequence.
>
> Saint Isaac, *Homily 32*

> In that day God will not judge us about psalmody, nor for the neglect of prayer, but because by abandoning them we have opened our door to the demons.
>
> Saint Isaac, *Homily 32*

> Just as thieves will not attack a place where they see royal weapons stacked, so he who has

united his heart to prayer will not lightly be raided by spiritual thieves.

Saint John of the Ladder, *Step 26:33*

As a companion, therefore, and an aid in the holy endeavour of prayer and spiritual watchfulness, we offer this *Prayer Book*.

A number of texts in the *Prayer Book* were set to the metre of the original Greek for our *Great Horologion*, printed in 1997. This second edition of the *Prayer Book* incorporates those metered versions, together with a handful of textual corrections.

This edition is printed in memory of Monk Athanasius and Nun Rebekah Xenia. May the Lord grant them rest in His Kingdom.

Pray for us, dear Christians, that we find mercy in the day of the Lord.

HOLY TRANSFIGURATION MONASTERY

September 1, 1987
Beginning of the Indiction
Saint Symeon the Stylite

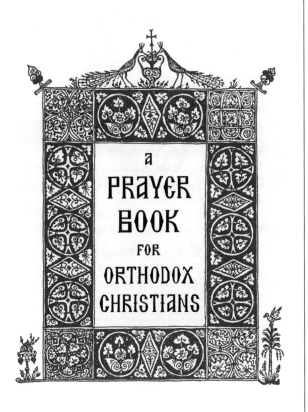

A
PRAYER
BOOK
FOR
ORTHODOX
CHRISTIANS

ΤΗΕ ΡΑΝΤΟCRΑΤΟR

RULER OF ALL

MORNING PRAYERS

On arising from sleep, stand before the holy icons with reverence and fear of God; make the sign of the Cross and say:

IN the Name of the Father, and of the Son, and of the Holy Spirit. Amen.

Then the introductory prayers:

Glory to Thee, our God, glory to Thee.

Heavenly King, O Comforter, the Spirit of truth, Who art everywhere present and fillest all things, O Treasury of every good and Bestower of life: come and dwell in us, and cleanse us from every stain, and save our souls, O Good One.

Holy God, Holy Mighty, Holy Immortal, have mercy on us. (3)

Glory to the Father, and to the Son, and to the Holy Spirit; both now and ever, and unto the ages of ages. Amen.

All-holy Trinity, have mercy on us. Lord, be

gracious unto our sins. Master, pardon our iniquities. Holy One, visit and heal our infirmities for Thy Name's sake.

Lord, have mercy. (3)

Glory to the Father, and to the Son, and to the Holy Spirit; both now and ever, and unto the ages of ages. Amen.

OUR Father, Which art in the Heavens, hallowed be Thy Name. Thy Kingdom come. Thy will be done, on earth as it is in Heaven. Give us this day our daily bread. And forgive us our debts, as we forgive our debtors. And lead us not into temptation, but deliver us from the evil one.

Through the prayers of our holy Fathers, Lord Jesus Christ our God, have mercy on us. Amen.

Then the following Troparia to the Holy Trinity:

AS we arise from sleep, we fall down before Thee, O Good One, and we cry unto Thee with the hymn of the Angels, O Mighty One: Holy, Holy, Holy art Thou, O God. Through the Theotokos, have mercy on us.

Glory.

HAVING raised me from bed and from sleep, O Lord, enlighten my mind and my heart, and open Thou my lips that I may praise Thee, O Holy Trinity. Holy, Holy, Holy art Thou, O God. Through the Theotokos, have mercy on us.

Both now.

OF a sudden the Judge shall come, and the deeds of each shall be laid bare. But let us cry out with fear in the midst of the night: Holy, Holy, Holy art Thou, O God. Through the Theotokos, have mercy on us.

Lord, have mercy. (12)

And the following prayer:

As I rise from sleep I thank Thee, O Holy Trinity, for because of Thy great goodness and long-suffering Thou wast not wroth with me, the slothful and sinner, nor didst Thou destroy me in mine iniquities, but didst show Thy wonted love for man, and when I was prostrate in despair, Thou didst raise me to keep the morning watch and glorify Thy dominion. And now enlighten Thou the eyes of my mind, open my mouth to meditate on Thy words and to understand Thy commandments, and to do Thy will, and to chant unto Thee in heartfelt confession, and praise Thine All-holy Name, of the Father, and of the Son, and of the Holy

Spirit, now and ever, and unto the ages of ages. Amen.

O come, let us worship and fall down before our King and God.

O come, let us worship and fall down before Christ, our King and God.

O come, let us worship and fall down before Him, Christ the King and our God.

PSALM 50

HAVE mercy on me, O God, according to Thy great mercy; and according to the multitude of Thy compassions blot out my transgression.

Wash me thoroughly from mine iniquity, and cleanse me from my sin.

For I know mine iniquity, and my sin is ever before me.

Against Thee only have I sinned and done this evil before Thee, that Thou mightest be justified in Thy words, and prevail when Thou art judged.

For behold, I was conceived in iniquities, and in sins did my mother bear me.

For behold, Thou hast loved truth; the hidden and secret things of Thy wisdom hast Thou made manifest unto me.

Thou shalt sprinkle me with hyssop, and I

shall be made clean; Thou shalt wash me, and I shall be made whiter than snow.

Thou shalt make me to hear joy and gladness; the bones that be humbled, they shall rejoice.

Turn Thy face away from my sins, and blot out all mine iniquities.

Create in me a clean heart, O God, and renew a right spirit within me.

Cast me not away from Thy presence, and take not Thy Holy Spirit from me.

Restore unto me the joy of Thy salvation, and with Thy governing Spirit establish me.

I shall teach transgressors Thy ways, and the ungodly shall turn back unto Thee.

Deliver me from blood-guiltiness, O God, Thou God of my salvation; my tongue shall rejoice in Thy righteousness.

O Lord, Thou shalt open my lips, and my mouth shall declare Thy praise.

For if Thou hadst desired sacrifice, I had given it; with whole-burnt offerings Thou shalt not be pleased.

A sacrifice unto God is a broken spirit; a heart that is broken and humbled God will not despise.

Do good, O Lord, in Thy good pleasure unto Sion, and let the walls of Jerusalem be builded.

Then shalt Thou be pleased with a sacrifice of

righteousness, with oblation and whole-burnt offerings.

Then shall they offer bullocks upon Thine altar.

THE CREED

I BELIEVE in one God, the Father Almighty, Maker of heaven and earth, and of all things visible and invisible;

And in one Lord, Jesus Christ, the Son of God, the Only-begotten, begotten of the Father before all ages; Light of Light, true God of true God; begotten, not made; being of one essence with the Father; by Whom all things were made;

Who for us men, and for our salvation, came down from the Heavens, and was incarnate of the Holy Spirit and the Virgin Mary, and became man;

And was crucified for us under Pontius Pilate, suffered and was buried;

And arose again on the third day according to the Scriptures;

And ascended into the Heavens, and sitteth at the right hand of the Father;

And shall come again, with glory, to judge both the living and the dead; Whose Kingdom shall have no end;

And in the Holy Spirit, the Lord, the Giver of life; Who proceedeth from the Father;

Who with the Father and the Son together is
worshipped and glorified; Who spake by the
Prophets;

In One, Holy, Catholic, and Apostolic
Church.

I confess one baptism for the remission of
sins.

I look for the resurrection of the dead,

And the life of the age to come. Amen.

A PRAYER
OF SAINT BASIL THE GREAT

THEE do we bless, Thou Most High God and
Lord of mercy, Who ever workest with us
deeds great and unfathomable, glorious and ex-
traordinary, whereof there is no number; Who
hast given unto us sleep for rest from our infirmity, and for repose of our much-toiling flesh.
We thank Thee that Thou hast not destroyed
us in our iniquities, but hast shown Thy wonted love for man, and though we were prostrate
in despair, Thou hast raised us up to glorify
Thy dominion. Wherefore, we beseech Thine
incomparable goodness: Enlighten the eyes of
our understanding and raise our mind from the
heavy sleep of slothfulness. Open our mouth
and fill it with Thy praise, that we may be able
undistracted to sing and chant and give thanks
unto Thee, Who art God glorified in all and by
all, the beginningless Father, with Thine Only-

begotten Son, and Thine All-holy and good and life-creating Spirit, now and ever, and unto the ages of ages. Amen.

MOST glorious, Ever-virgin, blessed Theotokos, present our prayer to thy Son and our God, and pray that through thee He would save our souls.

MY hope is the Father, my refuge the Son, my shelter the Holy Spirit. O Holy Trinity, glory be to Thee.

UNTO thee do I commit mine every hope, O Mother of God; guard me under thy shelter.

IT is truly meet to call thee blest, the Theotokos, the ever-blessed and all-immaculate and Mother of our God. More honourable than the Cherubim, and beyond compare more glorious than the Seraphim, thee who without corruption gavest birth to God the Word, the very Theotokos, thee do we magnify.

FORGIVE them that hate us and do us wrong, O Lord; do good unto them that do good unto us. To our brethren and kinsmen, grant their requests that are unto salvation and life everlasting. Visit them that be in sickness, and grant them healing. Pilot them that be at sea. Accompany them that journey. Be Thou the ally of Orthodox Christians. Unto them that minister and show mercy unto us, grant forgiveness of sins. Upon them that have enjoined us, the unworthy, to pray for them, have mercy, according to Thy great mercy. Remember, O Lord, all our fathers and brethren who are gone to their rest before us, and grant them rest where the light of Thy countenance shineth. Remember, O Lord, our brethren who are in captivity, and deliver them from every misfortune. Remember, O Lord, them that bring oblations and do good works in Thy holy churches, and grant them their requests that are unto salvation and life everlasting. Remember, O Lord, us also, Thy humble and sinful and unworthy servants, and enlighten our mind with the light of Thy knowledge, and lead us in the path of Thy commandments; by the intercessions of Thine all-immaculate Mother, our Lady the Theotokos and Ever-virgin Mary, and of all Thy Saints, for blessed art Thou unto all ages of ages. Amen.

THE PRAYER
OF SAINT EPHRAIM THE SYRIAN

This prayer is said during the Holy and Great Fast, except on Saturdays and Sundays.

O Lord and Master of my life, a spirit of idleness, curiosity, ambition, and idle talk, give me not. (*Prostration*)

But a spirit of chastity, humility, patience, and love, bestow upon me, Thy servant. (*Prostration*)

Yea, O Lord King, grant me to see mine own failings and not to condemn my brother; for blessed art Thou unto the ages of ages. Amen. (*Prostration*)

Then we make twelve bows, after which we repeat the concluding verse of the prayer:

Yea, O Lord King, grant me to see mine own failings and not to condemn my brother; for blessed art Thou unto the ages of ages. Amen. (*Prostration*)

And at the last, say:

Through the prayers of our holy Fathers, Lord Jesus Christ our God, have mercy on us. Amen.

PRAYERS AT MEALTIME

BEFORE THE MIDDAY MEAL

OUR Father, Which art in the Heavens, hallowed be Thy Name. Thy Kingdom come. Thy will be done, on earth as it is in Heaven. Give us this day our daily bread. And forgive us our debts, as we forgive our debtors. And lead us not into temptation, but deliver us from the evil one.

Glory to the Father, and to the Son, and to the Holy Spirit; both now and ever, and unto the ages of ages. Amen.

Lord, have mercy. (3)

If a priest is present, he saith the blessing:

O Christ our God, bless the food and drink of Thy servants, for Thou art holy, always, now and ever, and unto the ages of ages. Amen.

But if there be no priest, say:

Through the prayers of our holy Fathers, Lord Jesus Christ our God, have mercy on us. Amen.

AFTER THE MIDDAY MEAL

WE thank Thee, O Christ our God, that Thou hast filled us with Thine earthly goods; deprive us not also of Thy Heavenly Kingdom, but as Thou camest in the midst of Thy disciples, O Saviour, and gavest them peace, come also amongst us and save us.

Glory to the Father, and to the Son, and to the Holy Spirit; both now and ever, and unto the ages of ages. Amen.

Lord, have mercy. (*3*)

If a priest is present, he saith the blessing after the meal:

Blessed is God Who hath mercy and nourisheth us from His abundant gifts, by His grace and love for man, always, now and ever, and unto the ages of ages. Amen.

But if there be no priest, say:

Through the prayers of our holy Fathers, Lord Jesus Christ our God, have mercy on us. Amen.

BEFORE THE EVENING MEAL

THE poor shall eat and be filled, and they that seek the Lord shall praise Him; their hearts shall live for ever and ever.

Glory to the Father, and to the Son, and to the Holy Spirit; both now and ever, and unto the ages of ages. Amen.

Lord, have mercy. (3)

If a priest is present, he saith the blessing:

O Christ our God, bless the food and drink of Thy servants, for Thou art holy, always, now and ever, and unto the ages of ages. Amen.

But if there be no priest, say:

Through the prayers of our holy Fathers, Lord Jesus Christ our God, have mercy on us. Amen.

AFTER THE EVENING MEAL

THOU hast gladdened us, O Lord, by Thy deeds, and in the works of Thy hands have we rejoiced.

The light of Thy countenance, O Lord, hath been signed upon us; Thou hast given gladness to our hearts.

From the fruit of wheat, wine, and oil have we been filled; in peace in the same place shall we lie down and sleep, for Thou, O Lord, alone hast made us to dwell in hope.

Glory to the Father, and to the Son, and to the Holy Spirit; both now and ever, and unto the ages of ages. Amen.

Lord, have mercy. (3)

If a priest is present, he saith the blessing after the meal:

God is with us, He that hath mercy and nourisheth us by His grace and love for man, always, now and ever, and unto the ages of ages. Amen.

But if there be no priest, say:

Through the prayers of our holy Fathers, Lord Jesus Christ our God, have mercy on us. Amen.

THE SERVICE OF
SMALL COMPLINE

Through the prayers of our holy Fathers, Lord Jesus Christ our God, have mercy on us. Amen.

Glory to Thee, our God, glory to Thee.

Heavenly King. *(For the complete text of the introductory prayers, see pages 17–18.)*

Holy God. All-holy Trinity. Our Father.

Through the prayers of our holy Fathers, Lord Jesus Christ our God, have mercy on us. Amen.

Lord, have mercy (12). Glory; both now.

O come, let us worship and fall down before our King and God.
O come, let us worship and fall down before Christ, our King and God.

O come, let us worship and fall down before Him, Christ the King and our God.

PSALM 50

HAVE mercy on me, O God, according to Thy great mercy; and according to the multitude of Thy compassions blot out my transgression.

Wash me thoroughly from mine iniquity, and cleanse me from my sin.

For I know mine iniquity, and my sin is ever before me.

Against Thee only have I sinned and done this evil before Thee, that Thou mightest be justified in Thy words, and prevail when Thou art judged.

For behold, I was conceived in iniquities, and in sins did my mother bear me.

For behold, Thou hast loved truth; the hidden and secret things of Thy wisdom hast Thou made manifest unto me.

Thou shalt sprinkle me with hyssop, and I shall be made clean; Thou shalt wash me, and I shall be made whiter than snow.

Thou shalt make me to hear joy and gladness; the bones that be humbled, they shall rejoice.

Turn Thy face away from my sins, and blot out all mine iniquities.

Create in me a clean heart, O God, and renew a right spirit within me.

Cast me not away from Thy presence, and take not Thy Holy Spirit from me.

Restore unto me the joy of Thy salvation, and with Thy governing Spirit establish me.

I shall teach transgressors Thy ways, and the ungodly shall turn back unto Thee.

Deliver me from blood-guiltiness, O God, Thou God of my salvation; my tongue shall rejoice in Thy righteousness.

O Lord, Thou shalt open my lips, and my mouth shall declare Thy praise.

For if Thou hadst desired sacrifice, I had given it; with whole-burnt offerings Thou shalt not be pleased.

A sacrifice unto God is a broken spirit; a heart that is broken and humbled God will not despise.

Do good, O Lord, in Thy good pleasure unto Sion, and let the walls of Jerusalem be builded.

Then shalt Thou be pleased with a sacrifice of righteousness, with oblation and whole-burnt offerings.

Then shall they offer bullocks upon Thine altar.

PSALM 69

O GOD, be attentive unto helping me; O Lord, make haste to help me.

Let them be shamed and confounded that seek after my soul.

Let them be turned back and brought to shame that desire evils against me.

Let them be turned back straightway in shame that say unto me: Well done! Well done!

Let them be glad and rejoice in Thee all that seek after Thee, O God, and let them that love Thy salvation say continually: The Lord be magnified.

But as for me, I am poor and needy; O God, come unto mine aid.

My helper and my deliverer art Thou, O Lord; make no long tarrying.

PSALM 142

O LORD, hear my prayer, give ear unto my supplication in Thy truth; hearken unto me in Thy righteousness.

And enter not into judgment with Thy servant, for in Thy sight shall no man living be justified.

For the enemy hath persecuted my soul; he hath humbled my life down to the earth.

He hath sat me in darkness as those that have been long dead, and my spirit within me is become despondent; within me my heart is troubled.

I remembered days of old, I meditated on all Thy works, I pondered on the creations of Thy hands.

I stretched forth my hands unto Thee; my soul thirsteth after Thee like a waterless land.

Quickly hear me, O Lord; my spirit hath fainted away.

Turn not Thy face away from me, lest I be like unto them that go down into the pit.

Cause me to hear Thy mercy in the morning; for in Thee have I put my hope.

Cause me to know, O Lord, the way wherein I should walk; for unto Thee have I lifted up my soul.

Rescue me from mine enemies, O Lord; unto Thee have I fled for refuge. Teach me to do Thy will, for Thou art my God.

Thy good Spirit shall lead me in the land of uprightness; for Thy Name's sake, O Lord, shalt Thou quicken me.

In Thy righteousness shalt Thou bring my soul out of affliction, and in Thy mercy shalt Thou utterly destroy mine enemies.

And Thou shalt cut off all them that afflict my soul, for I am Thy servant.

DOXOLOGY

GLORY to God in the highest, and on earth peace, good will towards men.

We praise Thee; we bless Thee; we worship Thee; we glorify Thee; we give thanks to Thee for Thy great glory:

O Lord, Heavenly King, God the Father Almighty, O Lord the Only-begotten Son, Jesus Christ, and the Holy Spirit.

O Lord God, Lamb of God, Son of the Father, that takest away the sin of the world: have mercy on us, Thou that takest away the sins of the world.

Receive our prayer, Thou that sittest at the right hand of the Father; and have mercy on us.

For Thou only art holy; Thou only art Lord, Jesus Christ, to the glory of God the Father. Amen.

Every day will I bless Thee, and I will praise Thy Name for ever, yea, for ever and ever.

Lord, Thou hast been our refuge from generation to generation. I said: O Lord, have mercy on me; heal my soul, for I have sinned against Thee.

Lord, unto Thee have I fled for refuge; teach me to do Thy will, for Thou art my God.

For in Thee is the fountain of life; in Thy light shall we see light.

O continue Thy mercy unto them that know Thee.

Vouchsafe, O Lord, to keep us this night without sin.

Blessed art Thou, O Lord, the God of our Fathers, and praised and glorified is Thy Name unto the ages. Amen.

Let Thy mercy, O Lord, be upon us, according as we have hoped in Thee.

Blessed art Thou, O Lord, teach me Thy statutes.

Blessed art Thou, O Master, grant me understanding of Thy statutes.

Blessed art Thou, O Holy One, enlighten me by Thy statutes.

O Lord, Thy mercy endureth for ever; disdain not the works of Thy hands.

Unto Thee is due praise, unto Thee is due song, unto Thee glory is due, to the Father, and to the Son, and to the Holy Spirit, now and ever, and unto the ages of ages. Amen.

THE CREED

I BELIEVE in one God, the Father Almighty, Maker of heaven and earth, and of all things visible and invisible;

And in one Lord, Jesus Christ, the Son of God, the Only-begotten, begotten of the Father before all ages; Light of Light, true God of true God; begotten, not made; being of one essence with the Father; by Whom all things were made;

Who for us men, and for our salvation, came down from the Heavens, and was incarnate of

the Holy Spirit and the Virgin Mary, and became man;

And was crucified for us under Pontius Pilate, suffered and was buried;

And arose again on the third day according
to the Scriptures;

And ascended into the Heavens, and sitteth
at the right hand of the Father;

And shall come again, with glory, to judge
both the living and the dead; Whose Kingdom
shall have no end;

And in the Holy Spirit, the Lord, the Giver
of life; Who proceedeth from the Father;
Who with the Father and the Son together is
worshipped and glorified; Who spake by the
Prophets;

In One, Holy, Catholic, and Apostolic
Church.

I confess one baptism for the remission of
sins.

I look for the resurrection of the dead,
And the life of the age to come. Amen.

*Here may be read a Canon or Akathist, after which
we complete the Service of Small Compline:*

IT is truly meet to call thee blest, the Theotokos, the ever-blessed and all-immaculate
and Mother of our God. More honourable than
the Cherubim, and beyond compare more glorious than the Seraphim, thee who without

corruption gavest birth to God the Word, the very Theotokos, thee do we magnify.

Holy God. All-holy Trinity. Our Father.

Through the prayers of our holy Fathers, Lord Jesus Christ our God, have mercy on us. Amen.

Then the Troparion of the day, or the following:

O GOD of our Fathers, ever dealing with us according to Thy gentleness: take not Thy mercy from us, but by their entreaties guide our life in peace.

ADORNED in the blood of Thy Martyrs throughout all the world as in purple and fine linen, Thy Church, through them, doth cry unto Thee, O Christ God: Send down Thy compassions upon Thy people; grant peace to Thy commonwealth, and great mercy to our souls.

Glory.

WITH the Saints grant rest, O Christ, to the souls of Thy servants, where there is neither pain, nor sorrow, nor sighing, but life unending.

Both now. *Theotokion*

BY the intercession, O Lord, of all the Saints and the Theotokos, do Thou grant us Thy peace and have mercy on us, since Thou alone art compassionate.

Then:

Lord, have mercy. (40)

THOU Who at all times and at every hour, in Heaven and on earth, art worshipped and glorified, O Christ God, Who art long-suffering, plenteous in mercy, most compassionate, Who lovest the righteous and hast mercy on sinners, Who callest all to salvation through the promise of good things to come: receive, O Lord, our prayers at this hour, and guide our life toward Thy commandments. Sanctify our souls, make chaste our bodies, correct our thoughts, purify our intentions, and deliver us from every sorrow, evil, and pain. Compass us about with Thy holy Angels, that, guided and guarded by their array, we may attain to the unity of faith, and the knowledge of Thine unapproachable glory; for blessed art Thou unto the ages of ages. Amen.

Lord, have mercy. (3)

Glory; both now.

MORE honourable than the Cherubim, and beyond compare more glorious than the

Seraphim, thee who without corruption gavest birth to God the Word, the very Theotokos, thee do we magnify.

Through the prayers of our holy Fathers, Lord Jesus Christ our God, have mercy on us. Amen.

Then:

Lord, have mercy. (12)

Save, help, and protect us, O Virgin Theotokos.

A PRAYER
TO THE MOST HOLY THEOTOKOS
By Paul, a monk of the Monastery of the Benefactress

O SPOTLESS, undefiled, incorrupt, immaculate, pure Virgin, Lady Bride of God, who by thy wondrous conceiving hast united God the Word to man, and joined the outcast nature of our race to heavenly things, O only hope of the hopeless, and succour of the embattled, the ready help of them that have recourse to thee, and refuge of all Christians: abhor me not, the sinner, the accursed one, who have altogether made myself unprofitable by shameful thoughts, words, and deeds, and with the heartsease of life's pleasures am become a thrall in mind. But as the Mother of

41

the man-befriending God, do thou, in man-befriending wise, take pity upon me a sinner and prodigal, and receive my supplication, offered thee on unclean lips. And using thy boldness as a mother, entreat thy Son, our Master and Lord, that He may open even unto me the loving compassions of His goodness, and that, overlooking mine innumerable trespasses, He would turn me to repentance, and make me the approved doer of His commandments. And be thou ever with me, as thou art merciful, and compassionate, and the lover of good, being in this life a fervent protectress and help, to defend me from the assaults of adversaries, and guide me unto salvation; and in the hour of my departure, to care for my wretched soul, and drive far from it the dark countenances of evil demons; and in the terrible day of judgment, to deliver me from eternal torment, and show me forth as an heir of the unspeakable glory of thy Son and our God. This be my lot, O my Lady, most holy Theotokos, by thy mediation and help, through the grace and love for man of thine Only-begotten Son, our Lord and God and Saviour Jesus Christ, to Whom is due all glory, honour, and worship, with His Father which is without beginning, and His All-holy and good and life-creating Spirit, now and ever, and unto the ages of ages. Amen.

A PRAYER
TO OUR LORD JESUS CHRIST
By Antiochus, a monk of Pandectis

AND grant us, O Master, when we go to sleep, repose of body and soul; and keep us from the murky slumbering of sin and every dark voluptuousness of night. Calm the violence of the passions, quench the fiery darts of the evil one, which are treacherously hurled against us. Subdue the rebellions of our flesh, and quell our every earthly and material thought. And grant unto us, O God, a watchful mind, a chaste thought, a sober heart, and sleep light and free from all satanic phantasies. And raise us up at the hour of prayer, established in Thy commandments and holding the remembrance of Thy judgments unshakeable within us. Grant us to hymn Thy glory all the night long, that we may praise and bless and glorify Thine all-honoured and majestical Name, of the Father, and of the Son, and of the Holy Spirit, now and ever, and unto the ages of ages. Amen.

MOST glorious, Ever-virgin, blessed Theotokos, present our prayer to thy Son and our God, and pray that through thee He would save our souls.

MY hope is the Father, my refuge the Son, my shelter the Holy Spirit. O Holy Trinity, glory be to Thee.

U NTO thee do I commit mine every hope, O Mother of God; guard me under thy shelter.

I N thee, O Full of Grace, all creation–both the company of Angels and the race of men–doth rejoice. O hallowed temple and spiritual paradise, boast of virgins: from thee God was incarnate, and became a child, He, our God, Who existed before the ages; for He made thy womb a throne, and He made thee more spacious than the heavens. In thee, O Full of Grace, all creation doth rejoice. Glory be to thee.

A PRAYER
TO THE GUARDIAN ANGEL

O HOLY Angel, attendant of my wretched soul and of mine afflicted life, forsake me not, a sinner, neither depart from me for mine incontinency. Give no place to the evil demon to subdue me with the oppression of this mortal body; but take me by my wretched and outstretched hand, and lead me in the way of salvation. Yea, O holy Angel of God, the guardian and protector of my hapless soul and body, forgive me all things whatsoever wherewith I have troubled thee, all the days of my life, and if I have sinned in anything this day. Shelter me in this present night, and keep me from every affront of the enemy, lest I anger

God by any sin; and intercede with the Lord in my behalf, that He might strengthen me in the fear of Him, and make me a worthy servant of His goodness. Amen.

O THEOTOKOS and Virgin, rejoice, O Mary, full of grace; the Lord is with thee. Blessed art thou among women, and blessed is the Fruit of thy womb; for thou hast borne the Saviour of our souls. (3)

Then the following Theotokion in Third Tone:

A WED by the beauty of thy virginity and the exceeding radiance of thy purity, Gabriel called out unto thee, O Theotokos: What worthy hymn of praise can I offer unto thee? And what shall I name thee? I am in doubt and stand in awe. Wherefore, as commanded, I cry to thee: Rejoice, O Full of Grace.

Through the prayers of our holy Fathers, Lord Jesus Christ our God, have mercy on us. Amen.

THE SERVICE OF
VESPERS

The priest: Blessed is our God, always, now and ever, and unto the ages of ages.

The reader: **Amen.** *But if there be no priest, then:* Through the prayers of our holy Fathers, Lord Jesus Christ our God, have mercy on us. Amen.

The priest, but if there be no priest, then the reader: Glory to Thee, our God, glory to Thee.

Heavenly King. (*For the complete text of the introductory prayers, see pages 17–18.*)

The reader: Holy God. All-holy Trinity. Our Father.

The priest: For Thine is the kingdom, and the power, and the glory, of the Father, and of the Son, and of the Holy Spirit, now and ever, and unto the ages of ages.

The reader: **Amen.** *But if there be no priest, then the reader:* Through the prayers of our holy Fathers,

Lord Jesus Christ our God, have mercy on us. Amen.

Lord, have mercy (12). Glory; both now.

O come, let us worship and fall down before our King and God.

O come, let us worship and fall down before Christ, our King and God.

O come, let us worship and fall down before Him, Christ the King and our God.

THE PROEMIAL PSALM
PSALM 103

BLESS the Lord, O my soul; O Lord my God, Thou hast been magnified exceedingly.

Confession and majesty hast Thou put on, Who coverest Thyself with light as with a garment,

Who stretchest out the heaven as it were a curtain; Who supporteth His chambers in the waters,

Who appointeth the clouds for His ascent, Who walketh upon the wings of the winds,

Who maketh His angels spirits, and His ministers a flame of fire,

Who establisheth the earth in the sureness thereof; it shall not be turned back for ever and ever.

The abyss like a garment is His mantle; upon the mountains shall the waters stand.

At Thy rebuke they will flee, at the voice of Thy thunder shall they be afraid.

The mountains rise up and the plains sink down, unto the place where Thou hast established them.

Thou appointedst a bound that they shall not pass, neither return to cover the earth.

He sendeth forth springs in the valleys; between the mountains will the waters run.

They shall give drink to all the beasts of the field; the wild asses will wait to quench their thirst.

Beside them will the birds of the heaven lodge, from the midst of the rocks will they give voice.

He watereth the mountains from His chambers; the earth shall be satisfied with the fruit of Thy works.

He causeth the grass to grow for the cattle, and green herb for the service of men,

To bring forth bread out of the earth; and wine maketh glad the heart of man.

To make his face cheerful with oil; and bread strengtheneth man's heart.

The trees of the plain shall be satisfied, the cedars of Lebanon, which Thou hast planted.

There will the sparrows make their nests; the house of the heron is chief among them.

The high mountains are a refuge for the harts, and so is the rock for the hares.

He hath made the moon for seasons; the sun knoweth his going down.

Thou appointedst the darkness, and there was the night, wherein all the beasts of the forest will go abroad.

Young lions roaring after their prey, and seeking their food from God.

The sun ariseth, and they are gathered together, and they lay them down in their dens.

But man shall go forth unto his work, and to his labour until the evening.

How magnified are Thy works, O Lord! In wisdom hast Thou made them all; the earth is filled with Thy creation.

So is this great and spacious sea, therein are things creeping innumerable, small living creatures with the great.

There go the ships; there this dragon, whom Thou hast made to play therein.

All things wait on Thee, to give them their food in due season; when Thou givest it them, they will gather it.

When Thou openest Thy hand, all things shall be filled with goodness; when Thou turnest away Thy face, they shall be troubled.

Thou wilt take their spirit, and they shall cease; and unto their dust shall they return.

Thou wilt send forth Thy Spirit, and they shall be created; and Thou shalt renew the face of the earth.

Let the glory of the Lord be unto the ages;
the Lord will rejoice in His works,

Who looketh on the earth and maketh it
tremble, Who toucheth the mountains and
they smoke.

I will sing unto the Lord throughout my life,
I will chant to my God for as long as I have my
being.

May my words be sweet unto Him, and I
will rejoice in the Lord.

O that sinners would cease from the earth,
and they that work iniquity, that they should
be no more. Bless the Lord, O my soul.

And again:

The sun knoweth his going down; Thou appointedst the darkness, and there was the night.

How magnified are Thy works, O Lord! In
wisdom hast Thou made them all.

Glory to the Father, and to the Son, and to
the Holy Spirit; both now and ever, and unto
the ages of ages. Amen.

Alleluia, alleluia, alleluia: Glory to Thee, O
God. (3)

Our Hope, O Lord, glory be to Thee.

THE GREAT LITANY

The deacon: In peace let us pray to the Lord....

The priest: For unto Thee is due all glory, honour, and worship, to the Father, and to the Son, and to the Holy Spirit, now and ever, and unto the ages of ages.

The choir: Amen.

Then the appointed Kathisma from the Psalter is read.

THE SMALL LITANY

The deacon: Again and again, in peace let us pray to the Lord. . . .

The priest: For Thine is the dominion, and Thine is the kingdom, and the power, and the glory, of the Father, and of the Son, and of the Holy Spirit, now and ever, and unto the ages of ages.

The choir: Amen.

PSALM 140

In the tone of the week or of the feast.

LORD, I have cried unto Thee, hearken unto me; hearken unto me, O Lord. Lord, I have cried unto Thee, hearken unto me; attend to the voice of my supplication when I cry unto Thee. Hearken unto me, O Lord.

Let my prayer be set forth as incense before Thee, the lifting up of my hands as an evening sacrifice. Hearken unto me, O Lord.

Set, O Lord, a watch before my mouth, and a door of enclosure round about my lips.

Incline not my heart unto words of evil, to make excuse with excuses in sins,

With men that work iniquity; and I will not join with their chosen.

The righteous man will chasten me with mercy and reprove me; as for the oil of the sinner, let it not anoint my head.

For yet more is my prayer in the presence of their pleasures; swallowed up near by the rock have their judges been.

They shall hear my words, for they be sweetened; as a clod of earth is broken upon the earth, so have their bones been scattered nigh unto Hades.

For unto Thee, O Lord, O Lord, are mine eyes, in Thee have I hoped; take not my soul away.

Keep me from the snare which they have laid for me, and from the stumbling-blocks of them that work iniquity.

The sinners shall fall into their own net; I am alone until I pass by.

PSALM 141

WITH my voice unto the Lord have I cried, with my voice unto the Lord have I made supplication.

I will pour out before Him my supplication, mine affliction before Him will I declare.

When my spirit was fainting within me, then Thou knewest my paths.

In this way wherein I have walked they hid for me a snare.

I looked upon my right hand, and beheld, and there was none that did know me.

Flight hath failed me, and there is none that watcheth out for my soul.

I have cried unto Thee, O Lord; I said: Thou art my hope, my portion art Thou in the land of the living.

Attend unto my supplication, for I am brought very low.

Deliver me from them that persecute me, for they are stronger than I.

The appointed hymns as indicated in the Typicon *are chanted in alternation with the final verses, according to the number of hymns.*

Bring my soul out of prison that I may confess Thy Name.

The righteous shall wait patiently for me until Thou shalt reward me.

PSALM 129

Out of the depths have I cried unto Thee, O Lord; O Lord, hear my voice.

Let Thine ears be attentive to the voice of my supplication.

If Thou shouldest mark iniquities, O Lord, O Lord, who shall stand? For with Thee there is forgiveness.

For Thy Name's sake have I patiently waited for Thee, O Lord; my soul hath waited patiently for Thy word, my soul hath hoped in the Lord.

From the morning watch until night, from the morning watch let Israel hope in the Lord.

For with the Lord there is mercy, and with Him is plenteous redemption; and He shall redeem Israel out of all his iniquities.

PSALM 116

O PRAISE the Lord, all ye nations; praise Him, all ye peoples.

For He hath made His mercy to prevail over us, and the truth of the Lord abideth for ever.

Glory to the Father, and to the Son, and to the Holy Spirit.

Then the Doxasticon is chanted, when one is appointed.

Both now and ever, and unto the ages of ages. Amen.

Then the appointed Theotokion is chanted.

The deacon: Wisdom. Upright.

THANKSGIVING
AT THE LIGHTING OF THE LAMPS

O JOYOUS Light of the holy glory of the immortal, heavenly, holy, blessed Father, O Jesus Christ: We that come to the setting of the sun, when we behold the evening light, praise Father, Son, and Holy Spirit, God. Meet it is for Thee at all times to be praised with gladsome voices, O Son of God, Giver of life. Wherefore, the world doth glorify Thee.

The deacon: Vespers Prokeimenon.

PROKEIMENA
For the evening of the Lord's Day
Plagal of Fourth Tone

Behold now, bless ye the Lord, all ye servants of the Lord.

Verse: Ye that stand in the house of the Lord, in the courts of the house of our God.

For Monday evening. Fourth Tone

The Lord will hearken unto me when I cry unto Him.

Verse: When I called upon Thee, O God of my righteousness, Thou didst hearken unto me.

For Tuesday evening. First Tone

Thy mercy shall pursue me, O Lord, all the days of my life.

Verse: The Lord is my shepherd, and I shall not want. In a place of green pasture, there hath He made me to dwell.

For Wednesday evening. Plagal of First Tone

O God, in Thy Name save me, and in Thy strength do Thou judge me.

Verse: O God, hearken unto my prayer, give ear unto the words of my mouth.

For Thursday evening. Plagal of Second Tone

My help cometh from the Lord, Who hath made heaven and the earth.

Verse: I have lifted up mine eyes to the mountains, from whence cometh my help.

For Friday evening. Grave Tone

O God, Thou art my helper; Thy mercy shall go before me.

Verse: Rescue me from mine enemies, O God, and from them that rise up against me redeem me.

For Saturday evening. Plagal of Second Tone

The Lord is King, He is clothed with majesty.

Verse: The Lord is clothed with strength and He hath girt Himself.

Verse: For He established the world which shall not be shaken.

Then follow the readings, if they are appointed.

The deacon: Let us all say with our whole soul and with our whole mind, let us say. . . .

The priest: For a merciful and man-befriending God art Thou, and unto Thee do we send up glory, to the Father, and to the Son, and to the Holy Spirit, now and ever, and unto the ages of ages.

The choir: Amen.

The reader:

VOUCHSAFE, O Lord, to keep us this evening without sin. Blessed art Thou, O Lord, the God of our Fathers, and praised and glorified is Thy Name unto the ages. Amen. Let Thy mercy, O Lord, be upon us, according as we have hoped in Thee. Blessed art Thou, O Lord, teach me Thy statutes. Blessed art Thou, O Master, grant me understanding of Thy statutes. Blessed art Thou, O Holy One, enlighten me by Thy statutes. O Lord, Thy mercy endureth for ever; disdain not the works of Thy hands. Unto Thee is due praise, unto Thee is due song, unto Thee glory is due, to the Father, and to the Son, and to the Holy Spirit, now and ever, and unto the ages of ages. Amen.

The deacon: Let us complete our evening prayer unto the Lord. . . .

The priest: For a good and man-befriending God art Thou, and unto Thee do we send up glory, to the Father, and to the Son, and to the Holy Spirit, now and ever, and unto the ages of ages.

The choir: Amen.

The priest: Peace be unto all.

The choir: And to thy spirit.

The deacon: Let us bow our heads unto the Lord.

The choir: To Thee, O Lord.

The priest: Blessed and glorified be the dominion of Thy Kingdom, of the Father, and of the Son, and of the Holy Spirit, now and ever, and unto the ages of ages.

The choir: Amen.

On the eve of a Great Feast, and on other days as may be appointed, there followeth the Service of Entreaty (Liti), before the Aposticha.

Then the Aposticha of the day are chanted.

THE PRAYER OF SAINT SYMEON

Now lettest Thou Thy servant depart in peace, O Master, according to Thy word, for mine eyes have seen Thy salvation, which Thou hast prepared before the face of all peoples: a light of revelation for the nations, and the glory of Thy people Israel.

The reader: Holy God. All-holy Trinity. Our Father.

The priest: For Thine is the kingdom, and the power, and the glory, of the Father, and of the Son, and of the Holy Spirit, now and ever, and unto the ages of ages.

The reader: **Amen.** *But if there be no priest, then the reader:* Through the prayers of our holy Fathers, Lord Jesus Christ our God, have mercy on us. Amen.

Then the Dismissal Hymn(s) of the day and the appointed Theotokion are chanted.

If Vespers is celebrated as part of a Vigil, and the Service of Entreaty hath been chanted, the Blessing of the Loaves followeth here.

The deacon: Let us pray to the Lord.

The choir: Lord, have mercy.

The priest: The blessing of the Lord and His mercy come upon you, by His divine grace and love for man, always, now and ever, and unto the ages of ages.

The choir: Amen.

If Vespers is celebrated as part of a Vigil, after the blessing of the priest there followeth an appointed reading, and straightway the reader beginneth the Six Psalms of Matins (page 68).

But if Vespers is not being celebrated as part of a Vigil, after the blessing of the priest, the reader saith this prayer:

The Lord God make steadfast the holy and blameless Faith of the pious and Orthodox Christians, with His holy Church and this city (*or* sacred monastery), unto the ages of ages. Amen.

The priest: Most holy Theotokos, save us.

The reader: More honourable than the Cherubim, and beyond compare more glorious than the Seraphim, thee who without corruption gavest birth to God the Word, the very Theotokos, thee do we magnify.

The priest: Glory to Thee, O God, our hope, glory to Thee.

The reader: Glory to the Father, and to the Son, and to the Holy Spirit; both now and ever, and unto the ages of ages. Amen.

Lord, have mercy (*3*). Holy Father, bless.

The priest:

HE that arose from the dead (*if it be the Lord's Day; or if it be a Feast of the Master, the appointed dismissal; but if not, then he beginneth:*) Christ our true God, by the intercessions of His all-immaculate and all-blameless holy Mother, by the power of the honoured and life-giving Cross, by the protection of the venerable, heavenly Bodiless Powers, by the supplications of the venerable, glorious Prophet, Forerunner, and Baptist John, of the holy, glorious, and all-famed Apostles, of the holy, glorious, victorious Martyrs, of our righteous and God-bearing Fathers, of (*the Saint to whom the temple is dedicated*), of the holy, righteous Ancestors of God Joachim and Anna, of (*the Saints of the day*), whose memory we celebrate, and of all the Saints—may He have mercy on us and save us, for He is good and the Friend of man.

Through the prayers of our holy Fathers, Lord Jesus Christ our God, have mercy on us.

The choir: Amen.

ĨC   X̃C

WHOSE
WINNOWING
FAN IS IN
HIS HAND

AND HE WILL
THOROUGHLY
PURGE HIS
FLOOR

THE SERVICE OF
MATINS

The priest: Blessed is our God, always, now and ever, and unto the ages of ages.

The reader: Amen. *But if there be no priest, then:* Through the prayers of our holy Fathers, Lord Jesus Christ our God, have mercy on us. Amen.

The priest, but if there be no priest, then the reader: Glory to Thee, our God, glory to Thee.

Heavenly King. (*For the complete text of the introductory prayers, see pages 17–18.*)

The reader: Holy God. All-holy Trinity. Our Father.

The priest: For Thine is the kingdom, and the power, and the glory, of the Father, and of the Son, and of the Holy Spirit, now and ever, and unto the ages of ages.

The reader: Amen. *But if there be no priest, then the reader:* Through the prayers of our holy Fathers,

Lord Jesus Christ our God, have mercy on us. Amen.

Lord, have mercy (12). Glory; both now.

O come, let us worship and fall down before our King and God.

O come, let us worship and fall down before Christ, our King and God.

O come, let us worship and fall down before Him, Christ the King and our God.

And the following Psalms:

PSALM 19

THE Lord hear thee in the day of affliction; the Name of the God of Jacob defend thee.

Let Him send forth unto thee help from His sanctuary, and out of Sion let Him help thee.

Let Him remember every sacrifice of thine, and thy whole-burnt offering let Him fatten.

The Lord grant thee according to thy heart, and fulfil all thy purposes.

We will rejoice in Thy salvation, and in the Name of the Lord our God shall we be magnified. The Lord fulfil all thy requests.

Now have I known that the Lord hath saved His anointed one; He will hearken unto him out of His holy Heaven; in mighty deeds is the salvation of His right hand.

Some trust in chariots, and some in horses,

but we will call upon the Name of the Lord our God.

They have been fettered and have fallen, but we are risen and are set upright.

O Lord, save the king, and hearken unto us in the day when we call upon Thee.

O LORD, in Thy strength the king shall be glad, and in Thy salvation shall he rejoice exceedingly.

The desire of his heart hast Thou granted unto him, and hast not denied him the requests of his lips.

Thou wentest before him with the blessings of goodness, Thou hast set upon his head a crown of precious stone.

He asked life of Thee, and Thou gavest him length of days unto ages of ages.

Great is his glory in Thy salvation; glory and majesty shalt Thou lay upon him.

For Thou shalt give him blessing for ever and ever, Thou shalt gladden him in joy with Thy countenance.

For the king hopeth in the Lord, and through the mercy of the Most High shall he not be shaken.

Let Thy hand be found on all Thine enemies; let Thy right hand find all that hate Thee.

For Thou wilt make them as an oven of fire in the time of Thy presence; the Lord in His wrath will trouble them sorely and fire shall devour them.

Their fruit wilt Thou destroy from the earth, and their seed from the sons of men.

For they have intended evil against Thee, they have devised counsels which they shall not be able to establish.

For Thou shalt make them turn their backs; among those that are Thy remnant, Thou shalt make ready their countenance.

Be Thou exalted, O Lord, in Thy strength; we will sing and chant of Thy mighty acts.

Glory to the Father, and to the Son, and to the Holy Spirit; both now and ever, and unto the ages of ages. Amen.

And we say:

Holy God. All-holy Trinity. Our Father.

The priest: For Thine is the kingdom, and the power, and the glory, of the Father, and of the Son, and of the Holy Spirit, now and ever, and unto the ages of ages.

The reader: Amen. *But if there be no priest, then the reader:* Through the prayers of our holy Fathers, Lord Jesus Christ our God, have mercy on us. Amen.

And the following Troparia:

Save, O Lord, Thy people, and bless Thine inheritance; grant Thou unto the faithful victory over adversaries. And by the power of Thy Cross do Thou preserve Thy commonwealth.

Glory.

Thou Who wast raised up on the Cross of Thine own will, O Christ our God, do Thou bestow Thy compassions upon this, Thy new commonwealth named after Thee. Gladden with Thy sovereign might our most Orthodox hierarchs, and vouchsafe them victory over every false teaching; and as Thy help in war may they possess the weapon of peace, the trophy invincible.

Both now. *Theotokion*

O dread protection that cannot be put to shame, disdain not, O good one, our entreaties, O all-hymned Theotokos. Make steadfast the commonwealth of the Orthodox; protect those whom thou hast enjoined to rule over us, and grant them victory from on high; for thou hast given birth to God, O only blessed one.

Then the priest saith:

Have mercy on us, O God, according to Thy great mercy: we pray Thee, hearken and have mercy.

The choir, after each petition:
Lord, have mercy. (3)

Again we pray for pious and Orthodox Christians.

Again we pray for our Bishop (*Name*), and all our brotherhood (*or* sisterhood) in Christ.

For a merciful and man-befriending God art Thou, and unto Thee do we send up glory, to the Father, and to the Son, and to the Holy Spirit, now and ever, and unto the ages of ages.

The reader: Amen. In the Name of the Lord, Father, bless.

The priest: Glory to the Holy, and Consubstantial, and Life-creating, and Indivisible Trinity, always, now and ever, and unto the ages of ages.

The reader: Amen.

And he beginneth the Six Psalms. (But note that if Vespers and Matins are celebrated as part of a Vigil, after the conclusion of Vespers and an appointed reading, straightway the reader beginneth:)

THE SIX PSALMS

GLORY to God in the highest, and on earth peace, good will towards men. (3)
O Lord, Thou shalt open my lips, and my mouth shall declare Thy praise. (2)

PSALM 3

O LORD, why are they multiplied that afflict me? Many rise up against me.

Many say unto my soul: There is no salvation for him in his God.

But Thou, O Lord, art my helper, my glory, and the lifter up of my head.

I cried unto the Lord with my voice, and He heard me out of His holy mountain.

I laid me down and slept; I awoke, for the Lord will help me.

I will not be afraid of ten thousands of people that set themselves against me round about.

Arise, O Lord, save me, O my God, for Thou hast smitten all who without cause are mine enemies; the teeth of sinners hast Thou broken.

Salvation is of the Lord, and Thy blessing is upon Thy people.

And again:

I laid me down and slept; I awoke, for the Lord will help me.

PSALM 37

O LORD, rebuke me not in Thine anger, nor chasten me in Thy wrath.

For Thine arrows are fastened in me, and Thou hast laid Thy hand heavily upon me.

There is no healing in my flesh in the face of Thy wrath; and there is no peace in my bones in the face of my sins.

For mine iniquities are risen higher than my head; as a heavy burden have they pressed heavily upon me.

My bruises are become noisome and corrupt in the face of my folly.

I have been wretched and utterly bowed down until the end; all the day long I went with downcast face.

For my loins are filled with mockings, and there is no healing in my flesh.

I am afflicted and humbled exceedingly, I have roared from the groaning of my heart.

O Lord, before Thee is all my desire, and my groaning is not hid from Thee.

My heart is troubled, my strength hath failed me; and the light of mine eyes, even this is not with me.

My friends and my neighbours drew nigh over against me and stood, and my nearest of kin stood afar off.

And they that sought after my soul used violence; and they that sought evils for me spake vain things, and craftinesses all the day long did they meditate.

But as for me, like a deaf man I heard them not, and was as a speechless man that openeth not his mouth.

And I became as a man that heareth not, and that hath in his mouth no reproofs.

For in Thee have I hoped, O Lord; Thou wilt hearken unto me, O Lord my God.

For I said: Let never mine enemies rejoice over me; yea, when my feet were shaken, those men spake boastful words against me.

For I am ready for scourges, and my sorrow is continually before me.

For I will declare mine iniquity, and I will take heed concerning my sin.

But mine enemies live and are made stronger than I, and they that hated me unjustly are multiplied.

They that render me evil for good slandered me, because I pursued goodness.

Forsake me not, O Lord my God, depart not from me.

Be attentive unto my help, O Lord of my salvation.

And again:

Forsake me not, O Lord my God, depart not from me.

Be attentive unto my help, O Lord of my salvation.

PSALM 62

O GOD, my God, unto Thee I rise early at dawn. My soul hath thirsted for Thee;

how often hath my flesh longed after Thee in a land barren and untrodden and unwatered.

So in the sanctuary have I appeared before Thee to see Thy power and Thy glory,

For Thy mercy is better than lives; my lips shall praise Thee.

So shall I bless Thee in my life, and in Thy Name will I lift up my hands.

As with marrow and fatness let my soul be filled, and with lips of rejoicing shall my mouth praise Thee.

If I remembered Thee on my bed, at the dawn I meditated on Thee.

For Thou art become my helper; in the shelter of Thy wings will I rejoice.

My soul hath cleaved after Thee, Thy right hand hath been quick to help me.

But as for these, in vain have they sought after my soul; they shall go into the nethermost parts of the earth, they shall be surrendered unto the edge of the sword; portions for foxes shall they be.

But the king shall be glad in God, everyone shall be praised that sweareth by Him; for the mouth of them is stopped that speak unjust things.

And again:

At the dawn I meditated on Thee, for Thou art become my helper; in the shelter of Thy wings will I rejoice.

My soul hath cleaved after Thee, Thy right hand hath been quick to help me.

The following prayers are said without bows or the sign of the Cross.

Glory to the Father, and to the Son, and to the Holy Spirit; both now and ever, and unto the ages of ages. Amen.

Alleluia, alleluia, alleluia: Glory to Thee, O God. (3)

Lord, have mercy. (3)

Glory to the Father, and to the Son, and to the Holy Spirit; both now and ever, and unto the ages of ages. Amen.

PSALM 87

O LORD God of my salvation, by day have I cried and by night before Thee.

Let my prayer come before Thee, bow down Thine ear unto my supplication,

For filled with evils is my soul, and my life unto Hades hath drawn nigh.

I am counted with them that go down into the pit; I am become as a man without help, free among the dead,

Like the bodies of the slain that sleep in the grave, whom Thou rememberest no more, and they are cut off from Thy hand.

They laid me in the lowest pit, in darkness and in the shadow of death.

Against me is Thine anger made strong, and all Thy billows hast Thou brought upon me.

Thou hast removed my friends afar from me; they have made me an abomination unto themselves.

I have been delivered up, and have not come forth; mine eyes are grown weak from poverty.

I have cried unto Thee, O Lord, the whole day long; I have stretched out my hands unto Thee.

Nay, for the dead wilt Thou work wonders? Or shall physicians raise them up that they may give thanks unto Thee?

Nay, shall any in the grave tell of Thy mercy, and of Thy truth in that destruction?

Nay, shall Thy wonders be known in that darkness, and Thy righteousness in that land that is forgotten?

But as for me, unto Thee, O Lord, have I cried; and in the morning shall my prayer come before Thee.

Wherefore, O Lord, dost Thou cast off my soul and turnest Thy face away from me?

A poor man am I, and in troubles from my youth; yea, having been exalted, I was humbled and brought to distress.

Thy furies have passed upon me, and Thy terrors have sorely troubled me.

They came round about me like water, all the day long they compassed me about together.

Thou hast removed afar from me friend and neighbour, and mine acquaintances because of my misery.

And again:

O Lord God of my salvation, by day have I cried and by night before Thee.

Let my prayer come before Thee, bow down Thine ear unto my supplication.

PSALM 102

Bless the Lord, O my soul, and all that is within me, bless His holy Name.

Bless the Lord, O my soul, and forget not all that He hath done for thee,

Who is gracious unto all thine iniquities, Who healeth all thine infirmities,

Who redeemeth thy life from corruption, Who crowneth thee with mercy and compassion,

Who fulfilleth thy desire with good things; thy youth shall be renewed as the eagle's.

The Lord performeth deeds of mercy, and executeth judgment for all them that are wronged.

He hath made His ways known unto Moses, unto the sons of Israel the things that He hath willed.

Compassionate and merciful is the Lord, long-suffering and plenteous in mercy; not unto the end will He be angered, neither unto eternity will He be wroth.

Not according to our iniquities hath He dealt with us, neither according to our sins hath He rewarded us.

For according to the height of heaven from the earth, the Lord hath made His mercy to prevail over them that fear Him.

As far as the east is from the west, so far hath He removed our iniquities from us.

Like as a father hath compassion upon his sons, so hath the Lord had compassion upon them that fear Him; for He knoweth whereof we are made, He hath remembered that we are dust.

As for man, his days are as the grass; as a flower of the field, so shall he blossom forth.

For when the wind is passed over it, then it shall be gone, and no longer will it know the place thereof.

But the mercy of the Lord is from eternity, even unto eternity, upon them that fear Him.

And His righteousness is upon sons of sons, upon them that keep His testament and remember His commandments to do them.

The Lord in Heaven hath prepared His throne, and His kingdom ruleth over all.

Bless the Lord, all ye His angels, mighty in strength, that perform His word, to hear the voice of His words.

Bless the Lord, all ye His hosts, His ministers that do His will.

Bless the Lord, all ye His works, in every place of His dominion. Bless the Lord, O my soul.

And again:

In every place of His dominion, bless the Lord, O my soul.

PSALM 142

O LORD, hear my prayer, give ear unto my supplication in Thy truth; hearken unto me in Thy righteousness.

And enter not into judgment with Thy servant, for in Thy sight shall no man living be justified.

For the enemy hath persecuted my soul; he hath humbled my life down to the earth.

He hath sat me in darkness as those that have been long dead, and my spirit within me is become despondent; within me my heart is troubled.

I remembered days of old, I meditated on all

Thy works, I pondered on the creations of Thy hands.

I stretched forth my hands unto Thee; my soul thirsteth after Thee like a waterless land.

Quickly hear me, O Lord; my spirit hath fainted away.

Turn not Thy face away from me, lest I be like unto them that go down into the pit.

Cause me to hear Thy mercy in the morning; for in Thee have I put my hope.

Cause me to know, O Lord, the way wherein I should walk; for unto Thee have I lifted up my soul.

Rescue me from mine enemies, O Lord; unto Thee have I fled for refuge. Teach me to do Thy will, for Thou art my God.

Thy good Spirit shall lead me in the land of uprightness; for Thy Name's sake, O Lord, shalt Thou quicken me.

In Thy righteousness shalt Thou bring my soul out of affliction, and in Thy mercy shalt Thou utterly destroy mine enemies.

And Thou shalt cut off all them that afflict my soul, for I am Thy servant.

And again:

Hearken unto me, O Lord, in Thy righteousness, and enter not into judgment with Thy servant. (2)

Thy good Spirit shall lead me in the land of uprightness.

Glory to the Father, and to the Son, and to the Holy Spirit; both now and ever, and unto the ages of ages. Amen.

Alleluia, alleluia, alleluia: Glory to Thee, O God. (3)
Our Hope, O Lord, glory be to Thee.

THE GREAT LITANY

The deacon: In peace let us pray to the Lord. . . .

The priest: For unto Thee is due all glory, honour, and worship, to the Father, and to the Son, and to the Holy Spirit, now and ever, and unto the ages of ages.

The choir: Amen.

Then God is the Lord *is chanted in the tone of the Dismissal Hymn of the day:*

G OD is the Lord, and hath appeared unto us; blessed is He that cometh in the Name of the Lord.

The foregoing hymn is repeated after each of the following verses:

Verse: O give thanks unto the Lord, and call upon His holy Name.

Verse: All the nations compassed me round

about, and by the Name of the Lord I warded them off.

Verse: This is the Lord's doing, and it is marvellous in our eyes.

And we chant the Dismissal Hymn(s) of the day and the appointed Theotokion.

Then the appointed Kathismata from the Psalter are read, and we chant the Sessional Hymns of the day after each Kathisma.

At the conclusion of the first Kathisma:

THE SMALL LITANY

The deacon: Again and again, in peace let us pray to the Lord. . . .

The priest: For Thine is the dominion, and Thine is the kingdom, and the power, and the glory, of the Father, and of the Son, and of the Holy Spirit, now and ever, and unto the ages of ages.

The choir: Amen.

At the conclusion of the second Kathisma, again the Small Litany, with the exclamation:

The priest: For a good and man-befriending God art Thou, and unto Thee do we send up glory, to the Father, and to the Son, and to the Holy Spirit, now and ever, and unto the ages of ages.

The choir: **Amen.**

For the third Kathisma, Psalm 118, **Blessed are the blameless,** *is read if it be the Lord's Day; or, if so appointed, the Polyeleos is chanted.*

Then, if it be the Lord's Day, the choir chanteth the following; but if not, continue on page 85.

THE EVLOGITARIA OF THE RESURRECTION
Plagal of First Tone

Blessed art Thou, O Lord, teach me Thy statutes.

THE assembly of Angels was amazed to see Thee accounted among the dead, Thou Who hadst destroyed the might of death, O Saviour, and didst raise up Adam with Thyself, and Who hadst freed all men from Hades.

Blessed art Thou, O Lord, teach me Thy statutes.

WHY do ye mingle myrrh with tears of compassion, O ye women disciples? The radiant Angel in the grave addressed the myrrh-bearing women: Behold the grave and exult, for the Saviour hath arisen from the sepulchre.

Blessed art Thou, O Lord, teach me Thy statutes.

AT early morn, the myrrh-bearers hastened to Thy sepulchre with lamentation; but an Angel came to them and said: The time for sorrow is ended; weep ye no longer. And tell the Apostles of the Resurrection.

Blessed art Thou, O Lord, teach me Thy statutes.

THE myrrh-bearing women came with myrrh unto Thy tomb, O Saviour, and they heard an Angel saying unto them: Why do ye count the Living among the dead? For, as God, He is risen from the sepulchre.

Glory. *Triadicon*

WE worship the Father, and His Son, and the Holy Spirit, the Holy Trinity, one in essence; and we cry out with the Seraphim: Holy, Holy, Holy art Thou, O Lord.

Both now. *Theotokion*

BY giving birth to the Giver of Life, O Virgin, thou didst rescue Adam from sin, and thou didst grant Eve joy instead of sorrow; for the God and Man Who was incarnate of thee guided back to life him that had fallen away therefrom.

Alleluia, alleluia, alleluia: Glory to Thee, O God. (*3*)

But on Saturdays, after Psalm 118 we chant:

THE EVLOGITARIA FOR THE REPOSED
Plagal of First Tone

Blessed art Thou, O Lord, teach me Thy statutes.

THE choir of the Saints hath found the Wellspring of life, and the Door of Paradise; I, too, have found the way by means of repentance; I am the lamb that was lost. Call me back again, O Saviour, and save me.

Blessed art Thou, O Lord, teach me Thy statutes.

YE that preached the Lamb of God, and like lambs yourselves did suffer slaughter, and were translated to a life that ageth not, O Saints, and is eternal; earnestly beseech Him, O Martyrs, and implore that we be granted loosing from debts.

Blessed art Thou, O Lord, teach me Thy statutes.

YE that have walked the narrow and afflicted way in life, and have taken up the Cross as a yoke, and have followed Me in faith: come ye and enjoy the prizes and celestial crowns that I have prepared for you.

Blessed art Thou, O Lord, teach me Thy statutes.

AN image am I of Thine ineffable glory, even though I bear the scars of stumblings. Have pity on Thy creature, O Master, and purify me in Thy compassion; and grant unto me that longed-for fatherland, making me again a citizen of Paradise.

Blessed art Thou, O Lord, teach me Thy statutes.

OF old Thou didst fashion me out of nothing and didst honour me with Thy divine image; but because of the transgression of the commandment, Thou didst return me again to the earth from which I was taken. Restore me again to Thy likeness that I may be refashioned in that ancient beauty.

Blessed art Thou, O Lord, teach me Thy statutes.

Do Thou grant rest, O God, unto Thy servants, and appoint a place for them in Paradise, wherein the choirs of Saints, O Lord, and the righteous shall shine forth as luminaries. To Thy servants that have fallen asleep do Thou grant rest, overlooking all their offences.

Glory. *Triadicon*

Let us praise the Trinal Radiance of the One Divinity piously, while crying: Holy art Thou, O Beginningless Father, Co-beginningless Son, and Divine Spirit. Do Thou enlighten us who worship Thee with faith, and snatch us away from the eternal fire.

Both now. *Theotokion*

Rejoice, O modest one, who didst give birth unto God in the flesh for the salvation of all, and through whom the race of man hath found salvation; through thee may we find Paradise, O pure and blessed Theotokos.

Alleluia, alleluia, alleluia: Glory to Thee, O God. (3)

And after the Polyeleos or the Evlogitaria, again the Small Litany, with the exclamation:

The priest: For blessed is Thy Name, and glorified is Thy Kingdom, of the Father, and of the Son, and of the Holy Spirit, now and ever, and unto the ages of ages.

The choir: Amen.

Then the Hypakoë, if it be the Lord's Day (but if not, the appointed Sessional Hymns), followed by the Hymns of Ascent and the Prokeimenon.

Then the deacon: Let us pray to the Lord.

The choir: Lord, have mercy.

The priest: For holy art Thou, O our God, Who restest in the holies, and unto Thee do we send up glory, to the Father, and to the Son, and to the Holy Spirit, now and ever, and unto the ages of ages.

The choir: Amen.

Then there is chanted:

Let every breath praise the Lord. (3)

And after this, the deacon saith: And that we may be deemed worthy to hear the holy Gospel, let us beseech the Lord our God.

The choir: Lord, have mercy. (3)

The deacon: Wisdom. Upright. Let us hear the holy Gospel.

The priest: Peace be unto all.

The choir: And to thy spirit.

The priest: The reading is from the holy Gospel according to Saint (*Name*).

The choir: Glory to Thee, O Lord, glory to Thee.

The deacon: Let us attend.

And the priest readeth the appointed Matinal Gospel.

The choir: Glory to Thee, O Lord, glory to Thee.

And after the Gospel, if it be the Lord's Day:

LET us who have beheld the Resurrection of Christ worship our holy Lord Jesus, Who is alone without sin. We worship Thy Cross, O Christ, and we praise and glorify Thy holy Resurrection. For Thou art our God, and we know none other beside Thee, and we call upon Thy Name. Come, all ye faithful, let us worship Christ's holy Resurrection, for behold, through the Cross joy hath come to the whole world. Forever blessing the Lord, we praise His Resurrection. He endured the Cross for us, and by death destroyed death.

Then the Fiftieth Psalm is chanted, if it be the Lord's Day; but on other days, it is simply read.

PSALM 50

HAVE mercy on me, O God, according to Thy great mercy; and according to the multitude of Thy compassions blot out my transgression.

Wash me thoroughly from mine iniquity, and cleanse me from my sin.

For I know mine iniquity, and my sin is ever before me.

Against Thee only have I sinned and done this evil before Thee, that Thou mightest be justified in Thy words, and prevail when Thou art judged.

For behold, I was conceived in iniquities, and in sins did my mother bear me.

For behold, Thou hast loved truth; the hidden and secret things of Thy wisdom hast Thou made manifest unto me.

Thou shalt sprinkle me with hyssop, and I shall be made clean; Thou shalt wash me, and I shall be made whiter than snow.

Thou shalt make me to hear joy and gladness; the bones that be humbled, they shall rejoice.

Turn Thy face away from my sins, and blot out all mine iniquities.

Create in me a clean heart, O God, and renew a right spirit within me.

Cast me not away from Thy presence, and take not Thy Holy Spirit from me.

Restore unto me the joy of Thy salvation, and with Thy governing Spirit establish me.

I shall teach transgressors Thy ways, and the ungodly shall turn back unto Thee.

Deliver me from blood-guiltiness, O God, Thou God of my salvation; my tongue shall rejoice in Thy righteousness.

O Lord, Thou shalt open my lips, and my mouth shall declare Thy praise.

For if Thou hadst desired sacrifice, I had given it; with whole-burnt offerings Thou shalt not be pleased.

A sacrifice unto God is a broken spirit; a heart that is broken and humbled God will not despise.

Do good, O Lord, in Thy good pleasure unto Sion, and let the walls of Jerusalem be builded.

Then shalt Thou be pleased with a sacrifice of righteousness, with oblation and whole-burnt offerings.

Then shall they offer bullocks upon Thine altar.

If it be the Lord's Day, we chant the following in Second Tone; but if it be a feast, the appointed hymns are chanted here.

Glory.

By the intercessions of the Apostles, O Merciful One, blot out the multitude of mine offences.

Both now. *Theotokion*

By the intercessions of the Theotokos, O Merciful One, blot out the multitude of mine offences.

Verse: Have mercy on me, O God, according to Thy great mercy; and according to the multitude of Thy compassions blot out my transgression.

Jesus, having risen from the grave as He foretold, hath granted us life everlasting and great mercy.

But if it be the period of the Triodion, *on the Lord's Day instead of the foregoing hymns, we chant the following:*

Glory. *Plagal of Fourth Tone*

Do Thou open unto me the doors of repentance, O Giver of Life; for my spirit goeth early unto Thy holy temple, bringing the temple of my body all defiled. But as One compassionate, cleanse me by Thy compassionate mercy.

Both now. *Theotokion*

Do thou make straight for me the paths of salvation, O Theotokos; for I have defiled my soul with shameful sins, having wasted my whole life in slothfulness. By thine intercessions, deliver me from all impurity.

Plagal of Second Tone

Verse: Have mercy on me, O God, according to Thy great mercy; and according to the multitude of Thy compassions blot out my transgression.

WHEN I, the hapless one, bring to mind the multitude of my terrible deeds, I tremble at the fearful day of judgment. But trusting in the mercy of Thy compassion, like David I cry to Thee: Have mercy on me, O God, according to Thy great mercy.

Then the deacon:

SAVE, O God, Thy people, and bless Thine inheritance; visit Thy world with mercy and compassions; exalt the horn of Orthodox Christians, and send down upon us Thy rich mercies: by the intercessions of our all-immaculate Lady Theotokos and Ever-virgin Mary; by the power of the honoured and life-giving Cross; by the protection of the venerable, heavenly Bodiless Powers; by the supplications of the venerable, glorious Prophet, Forerunner, and Baptist John; of the holy, glorious, and all-famed Apostles; of our Fathers among the

Saints, the great Hierarchs and universal Teachers, Basil the Great, Gregory the Theologian, and John Chrysostom; Athanasius, Cyril, and John the Almsgiver, Patriarchs of Alexandria; Nicholas, Archbishop of Myra, and Spyridon, Bishop of Trimythus, the wonderworkers; of the holy, glorious Great Martyrs, George the Trophy-bearer, Demetrius the Myrrh-streamer, Theodore the Tyro, Theodore the Commander, and Menas the wonderworker; of the Sacred Martyrs Haralampus and Eleutherius; of the holy, glorious, and triumphantly victorious Martyrs; of our righteous and God-bearing Fathers; of *(the Saint to whom the temple is dedicated)*; of the holy, righteous Ancestors of God Joachim and Anna; of *(the Saints of the day)* whose memory we keep, and of all Thy Saints: We beseech Thee, Thou only greatly merciful God, hearken unto us sinners who pray unto Thee, and have mercy on us.

The choir: **Lord, have mercy.** (12)

The priest: **By the mercy and compassions and love for man of Thine Only-begotten Son, with Whom Thou art blessed, together with Thine All-holy and good and life-creating Spirit, now and ever, and unto the ages of ages.**

The choir: **Amen.**

And we begin the appointed Canons. After the third Ode, the deacon saith the Small Litany, with the exclamation:

The priest: For thou art our God, and unto Thee do we send up glory, to the Father, and to the Son, and to the Holy Spirit, now and ever, and unto the ages of ages.

The choir: Amen.

Then the Sessional Hymn from the Menaion, and the fourth, fifth, and sixth Odes of the Canons. After the sixth Ode, the deacon saith the Small Litany, with the exclamation:

The priest: For Thou art the King of Peace, and the Saviour of our souls, and unto Thee do we send up glory, to the Father, and to the Son, and to the Holy Spirit, now and ever, and unto the ages of ages.

The choir: Amen.

Then the Kontakion and the Oikos, and the reading from the Synaxarion. Then the remaining Odes of the Canons. After the Katavasia of the eighth Ode, the deacon saith:

Let us magnify the Theotokos and Mother of the Light, honouring her with hymns.

And straightway the choir chanteth the Song of the Theotokos; but if it be a Feast of the Master or of the Mother of God, the ninth ode of the Canon is chanted instead.

THE SONG OF THE THEOTOKOS

M<small>Y</small> soul doth magnify the Lord, and my spirit hath rejoiced in God my Saviour.

The refrain, chanted after each of the verses:

M<small>ORE</small> honourable than the Cherubim, and beyond compare more glorious than the Seraphim, thee who without corruption gavest birth to God the Word, the very Theotokos, thee do we magnify.

For He hath looked upon the lowliness of His handmaiden; for behold, from henceforth all generations shall call me blessed.

For the Mighty One hath done great things to me, and holy is His Name; and His mercy is on them that fear Him unto generation and generation.

He hath showed strength with His arm, He hath scattered the proud in the imagination of their heart.

He hath put down the mighty from their seat, and exalted them of low degree; He hath filled the hungry with good things, and the rich He hath sent empty away.

He hath holpen His servant Israel in remembrance of His mercy, as He spake to our fathers, to Abraham and his seed for ever.

And after the Katavasia of the ninth Ode, the deacon saith the Small Litany, with the exclamation:

The priest: For all the hosts of the Heavens praise Thee, and unto Thee do they send up glory, to the Father, and to the Son, and to the Holy Spirit, now and ever, and unto the ages of ages.

The choir: Amen.

Then, if it be the Lord's Day:

Holy is the Lord our God. (3)
Exalt ye the Lord our God, and worship the footstool of His feet; for He is holy.

Then the Exapostilarion, with its appointed Theotokion. And straightway the Praises:

PSALM 148

LET every breath praise the Lord. Praise the Lord from the Heavens, praise Him in the highest. To Thee is due praise, O God.

Praise Him, all ye His angels; praise Him, all ye His hosts. To Thee is due praise, O God.

Praise Him, O sun and moon; praise Him, all ye stars and light.

Praise Him, ye heavens of heavens, and thou water that art above the heavens.

Let them praise the Name of the Lord; for

He spake, and they came to be; He commanded, and they were created.

He established them for ever, yea, for ever and ever; He hath set an ordinance, and it shall not pass away.

Praise the Lord from the earth, ye dragons, and all ye abysses,

Fire, hail, snow, ice, blast of tempest, which perform His word,

The mountains and all the hills, fruitful trees, and all cedars,

The beasts and all the cattle, creeping things and winged birds,

Kings of the earth, and all peoples, princes and all the judges of the earth,

Young men and virgins, elders with the younger; let them praise the Name of the Lord, for exalted is the Name of Him alone.

His praise is above the earth and heaven, and He shall exalt the horn of His people.

This is the hymn for all His saints, for the sons of Israel, and for the people that draw nigh unto Him.

PSALM 149

SING unto the Lord a new song; His praise is in the church of the saints.

Let Israel be glad in Him that made him, let the sons of Sion rejoice in their King.

Let them praise His Name in the dance; with the timbrel and the psaltery let them chant unto Him.

For the Lord taketh pleasure in His people, and He shall exalt the meek with salvation.

The saints shall boast in glory, and they shall rejoice upon their beds.

The high praise of God shall be in their throat, and two-edged swords shall be in their hands,

To do vengeance among the heathen, punishments among the peoples,

To bind their kings with fetters, and their nobles with manacles of iron,

The appointed hymns as indicated in the Typicon *are chanted in alternation with the final verses, according to the number of hymns.*

To do among them the judgment that is written. This glory shall be to all His saints.

PSALM 150

PRAISE ye God in His saints, praise Him in the firmament of His power.

Praise Him for His mighty acts, praise Him according to the multitude of His greatness.

Praise Him with the sound of trumpet, praise Him with the psaltery and harp.

Praise Him with timbrel and dance, praise Him with strings and flute.

Praise Him with tuneful cymbals, praise Him with cymbals of jubilation. Let every breath praise the Lord.

If it be the Lord's Day, these two verses are also chanted:

Arise, O Lord my God, let Thy hand be lifted high; forget not Thy paupers to the end.

I will confess Thee, O Lord, with my whole heart; I will tell of all Thy wonders.

Glory to the Father, and to the Son, and to the Holy Spirit.

The appointed Doxasticon.

Both now and ever, and unto the ages of ages. Amen.

The appointed Theotokion. If it be the Lord's Day:

MOST blessed art thou, O Virgin Theotokos; for through Him Who was incarnate of thee, Hades was taken captive, Adam was recalled, the curse was annulled. Eve was freed, death was put to death, and we were brought to life. Wherefore, with hymns we cry aloud: Blessed art Thou, O Christ our God, Who hast been thus well pleased; glory be to Thee.

And straightway we chant:

THE GREAT DOXOLOGY

GLORY to Thee, Who hast shown forth the light. Glory to God in the highest, and on earth peace, good will towards men.

We praise Thee; we bless Thee; we worship Thee; we glorify Thee; we give thanks to Thee for Thy great glory:

O Lord, Heavenly King, God the Father Almighty, O Lord the Only-begotten Son, Jesus Christ, and the Holy Spirit.

O Lord God, Lamb of God, Son of the Father, that takest away the sin of the world: have mercy on us, Thou that takest away the sins of the world.

Receive our prayer, Thou that sittest at the right hand of the Father; and have mercy on us.

For Thou only art holy; Thou only art Lord, Jesus Christ, to the glory of God the Father. Amen.

Every day will I bless Thee, and I will praise Thy Name for ever, yea, for ever and ever.

Vouchsafe, O Lord, to keep us this day without sin.

Blessed art Thou, O Lord, the God of our Fathers, and praised and glorified is Thy Name unto the ages. Amen.

Let Thy mercy, O Lord, be upon us, according as we have hoped in Thee.

Blessed art Thou, O Lord, teach me Thy statutes. (3)

Lord, Thou hast been our refuge from generation to generation. I said: O Lord, have mercy on me; heal my soul, for I have sinned against Thee.

Lord, unto Thee have I fled for refuge; teach me to do Thy will, for Thou art my God.

For in Thee is the fountain of life; in Thy light shall we see light.

O continue Thy mercy unto them that know Thee.

Holy God, Holy Mighty, Holy Immortal, have mercy on us. (3)

Glory to the Father, and to the Son, and to the Holy Spirit;

Both now and ever, and unto the ages of ages. Amen.

Holy Immortal, have mercy on us.

Holy God, Holy Mighty, Holy Immortal, have mercy on us.

Then the appointed Dismissal Hymn of the feast is chanted. On the Lord's Day, if the tone of the week be First, Second, Third, or Fourth, we chant:

Fourth Tone

TODAY is salvation come unto the world. Let us sing unto the Author of our life Who arose from the grave; for, destroying death by death, He granted us the victory and great mercy.

But if the tone of the week be Plagal of First, Plagal of Second, Grave, or Plagal of Fourth, we chant:

Plagal of Fourth Tone

RISING from the tomb and breaking the bonds of Hades asunder, Thou didst loose the sentence of death, O Lord, thereby delivering all men from the snares of the enemy. Manifesting Thyself to Thy disciples, Thou didst send them forth to preach, and through them Thou didst grant peace to the whole world, O Thou Who alone art rich in mercy.

Then:

The deacon: Have mercy on us, O God, according to Thy great mercy, we pray Thee, hearken and have mercy. . . .

The priest: For a merciful and man-befriending God art Thou, and unto Thee do we send up glory, to the Father, and to the Son, and to the Holy Spirit, now and ever, and unto the ages of ages.

The choir: Amen.

The deacon: Let us complete our morning prayer unto the Lord. . . .

The priest: For a God of mercies and compassions and love for man art Thou, and unto Thee do we send up glory, to the Father, and to the Son, and to the Holy Spirit, now and ever, and unto the ages of ages.

The choir: Amen.

The priest: Peace be unto all.

The choir: And to thy spirit.

The deacon: Let us bow our heads unto the Lord.

The choir: To Thee, O Lord.

The priest: For Thine it is to have mercy and to save us, O our God, and unto Thee do we send up glory, to the Father, and to the Son, and to the Holy Spirit, now and ever, and unto the ages of ages.

The choir: Amen.

The deacon: Wisdom.

The choir: Holy Father, bless.

The priest: Blessed is He that is, even Christ our God, always, now and ever, and unto the ages of ages.

The choir: Amen.

The reader: The Lord God make steadfast the

holy and blameless Faith of the pious and Orthodox Christians, with His holy Church and this city (*or* sacred monastery) unto the ages of ages. Amen.

The priest: Most holy Theotokos, save us.

The reader: More honourable than the Cherubim, and beyond compare more glorious than the Seraphim, thee who without corruption gavest birth to God the Word, the very Theotokos, thee do we magnify.

The priest: Glory to Thee, O God, our hope, glory to Thee.

The reader: Glory to the Father, and to the Son, and to the Holy Spirit; both now and ever, and unto the ages of ages. Amen.

Lord, have mercy (*3*). Holy Father, bless.

The priest:

H E that arose from the dead (*if it be the Lord's Day; or if it be a Feast of the Master, the appointed dismissal; but if not, then he beginneth:*) Christ our true God, by the intercessions of His all-immaculate and all-blameless holy Mother, by the power of the honoured and life-giving Cross, by the protection of the venerable, heavenly Bodiless Powers, by the supplications of the venerable, glorious Prophet, Forerunner, and Baptist John, of the holy, glorious, and all-famed Apostles, of the holy, glorious, victorious Martyrs, of our righteous and God-bearing Fathers, of *(the Saint to whom the temple is dedicated)*, of the holy, righteous Ancestors of God Joachim and Anna, of *(the Saints of the day)*, whose memory we celebrate, and of all the Saints—may He have mercy on us and save us, for He is good and the Friend of man.

Through the prayers of our holy Fathers, Lord Jesus Christ our God, have mercy on us.

The choir: **Amen.**

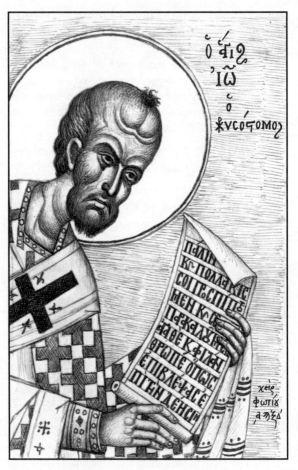

SAINT JOHN CHRYSOSTOM

THE DIVINE LITURGY

The deacon: Bless, Master.

The priest:

BLESSED is the Kingdom of the Father, and of the Son, and of the Holy Spirit, now and ever, and unto the ages of ages.

The choir: Amen.

THE GREAT LITANY

The deacon: In peace let us pray to the Lord.

The choir, after each petition: Lord, have mercy.

The deacon: For the peace from above, and the salvation of our souls, let us pray to the Lord.

For the peace of the whole world, the good estate of the holy churches of God, and the union of all the faithful, let us pray to the Lord.

For this holy house, and for them that with faith, reverence, and fear of God enter herein, let us pray to the Lord.

For our Bishop (*Name*), for the venerable Presbytery, the Diaconate in Christ, for all the clergy and the people, let us pray to the Lord.

For (*the title of the head of state*) and all civil authorities, that they may govern in peace and justice, let us pray to the Lord.

That He may aid them and grant them victory over every enemy and adversary, let us pray to the Lord.

For this city (*or* this sacred monastery), for every city and countryside, and the faithful that dwell therein, let us pray to the Lord.

For seasonable weather, abundance of the fruits of the earth, and peaceful times, let us pray to the Lord.

For them that travel by sea, land, and air, for the sick, the afflicted, for captives, and their salvation, let us pray to the Lord.

For our deliverance from all tribulation, wrath, danger, and necessity, let us pray to the Lord.

Help us, save us, have mercy on us, and keep us, O God, by Thy grace.

The choir: Amen.

Calling to remembrance our all-holy, immaculate, most blessed, glorious Lady Theotokos and Ever-virgin Mary with all the Saints, let us commit ourselves and one another and all our life unto Christ our God.

The choir: To Thee, O Lord.

The priest: For unto Thee is due all glory, honour, and worship, to the Father, and to the Son, and to the Holy Spirit, now and ever, and unto the ages of ages.

The choir: Amen.

FIRST STASIS OF THE TYPICA
PSALM 102

BLESS the Lord, O my soul; blessed art Thou, O Lord. Bless the Lord, O my soul, and all that is within me, bless His holy Name.

Bless the Lord, O my soul, and forget not all that He hath done for thee,

Who is gracious unto all thine iniquities, Who healeth all thine infirmities,

Who redeemeth thy life from corruption, Who crowneth thee with mercy and compassion,

Who fulfilleth thy desire with good things; thy youth shall be renewed as the eagle's.

The Lord performeth deeds of mercy, and executeth judgment for all them that are wronged.

He hath made His ways known unto Moses, unto the sons of Israel the things that He hath willed.

Compassionate and merciful is the Lord, long-suffering and plenteous in mercy; not unto the end will He be angered, neither unto eternity will He be wroth.

Not according to our iniquities hath He dealt with us, neither according to our sins hath He rewarded us.

For according to the height of heaven from the earth, the Lord hath made His mercy to prevail over them that fear Him.

As far as the east is from the west, so far hath He removed our iniquities from us.

Like as a father hath compassion upon his sons, so hath the Lord had compassion upon them that fear Him; for He knoweth whereof we are made, He hath remembered that we are dust.

As for man, his days are as the grass; as a flower of the field, so shall he blossom forth.

For when the wind is passed over it, then it shall be gone, and no longer will it know the place thereof.

But the mercy of the Lord is from eternity, even unto eternity, upon them that fear Him.

And His righteousness is upon sons of sons, upon them that keep His testament and remember His commandments to do them.

The Lord in Heaven hath prepared His throne, and His kingdom ruleth over all.

Bless the Lord, all ye His angels, mighty in

strength, that perform His word, to hear the voice of His words.

Bless the Lord, all ye His hosts, His ministers that do His will.

Bless the Lord, all ye His works, in every place of His dominion. Bless the Lord, O my soul.

Glory to the Father, and to the Son, and to the Holy Spirit;

Both now and ever, and unto the ages of ages. Amen.

Bless the Lord, O my soul, and all that is within me, bless His holy Name; blessed art Thou, O Lord.

THE SMALL LITANY

The deacon: Again and again, in peace let us pray to the Lord.

The choir: Lord, have mercy.

The deacon: Help us, save us, have mercy on us, and keep us, O God, by Thy grace.

The choir: Amen.

Calling to remembrance our all-holy, immaculate, most blessed, glorious Lady Theotokos and Ever-virgin Mary with all the Saints, let us commit ourselves and one another and all our life unto Christ our God.

The choir: To Thee, O Lord.

The priest: For Thine is the dominion, and Thine is the kingdom, and the power, and the glory, of the Father, and of the Son, and of the Holy Spirit, now and ever, and unto the ages of ages.

The choir: Amen.

SECOND STASIS OF THE TYPICA
PSALM 145

Glory to the Father, and to the Son, and to the Holy Spirit.

PRAISE the Lord, O my soul. I will praise the Lord in my life, I will chant unto my God for as long as I have my being.

Trust ye not in princes, in the sons of men, in whom there is no salvation.

His spirit shall go forth, and he shall return unto his earth.

In that day all his thoughts shall perish.

Blessed is he of whom the God of Jacob is his help, whose hope is in the Lord his God,

Who hath made heaven and the earth, the sea and all that is therein,

Who keepeth truth unto eternity, Who executeth judgment for the wronged, Who giveth food unto the hungry.

The Lord looseth the fettered; the Lord maketh wise the blind; the Lord setteth aright the fallen; the Lord loveth the righteous; the Lord preserveth the proselytes.

He shall adopt for His own the orphan and widow, and the way of sinners shall He destroy.

The Lord shall be king unto eternity; thy God, O Sion, unto generation and generation.

Both now and ever, and unto the ages of ages. Amen.

ONLY-BEGOTTEN Son and Word of God, Thou Who art immortal, and didst deign for our salvation to become incarnate of the holy Theotokos and Ever-virgin Mary, without change becoming man, and Who wast crucified, O Christ God, trampling down death by death: Thou Who art one of the Holy Trinity, glorified together with the Father and the Holy Spirit, save us.

THE SMALL LITANY

The deacon: Again and again, in peace let us pray to the Lord.

The choir: Lord, have mercy.

The deacon: Help us, save us, have mercy on us, and keep us, O God, by Thy grace.

The choir: Amen.

Calling to remembrance our all-holy, immaculate, most blessed, glorious Lady Theotokos and Ever-virgin Mary with all the Saints, let us commit ourselves and one another and all our life unto Christ our God.

The choir: To Thee, O Lord.

The priest: For a good and man-befriending God art Thou, and unto Thee do we send up glory, to the Father, and to the Son, and to the Holy Spirit, now and ever, and unto the ages of ages.

The choir: Amen.

THIRD STASIS OF THE TYPICA
THE BEATITUDES

The appointed hymns as indicated in the Typicon are chanted in alternation with the final verses of the Beatitudes, according to the number of hymns.

IN Thy Kingdom remember us, O Lord, when Thou comest in Thy Kingdom.

Blessed are the poor in spirit, for theirs is the Kingdom of the Heavens.

Blessed are they that mourn, for they shall be comforted.

Blessed are the meek, for they shall inherit the earth.

Blessed are they that hunger and thirst after righteousness, for they shall be filled.

Blessed are the merciful, for they shall obtain mercy.

Blessed are the pure in heart, for they shall see God.

Blessed are the peacemakers, for they shall be called sons of God.

Blessed are they that are persecuted for righteousness' sake, for theirs is the Kingdom of the Heavens.

Blessed are ye when men shall revile and persecute you and say all manner of evil against you falsely for My sake.

Rejoice and be glad, for your reward is great in the Heavens.

Glory to the Father, and to the Son, and to the Holy Spirit;

Both now and ever, and unto the ages of ages. Amen.

THE SMALL ENTRANCE

The deacon: Wisdom. Upright.

Then the following (unless it be a Feast of the Master, at which time the appointed Entrance Hymn is chanted instead):

COME, let us worship and fall down before Christ. O Son of God, Who art wondrous in the Saints (*or, if it be the Lord's Day,* Who didst arise from the dead), save us who chant to Thee: Alleluia.

Then the appointed Dismissal Hymns and Kontakia are chanted. Outside of periods of Great Feasts of the Master and of the Theotokos, the following is chanted as the last Kontakion:

O PROTECTION of Christians that cannot be put to shame, mediation unto the Creator most constant: O despise not the suppliant voices of those who have sinned; but be thou quick, O good one, to come unto our aid, who in faith cry unto thee: Hasten to intercession, and speed thou to make supplication, thou who dost ever protect, O Theotokos, them that honour thee.

The deacon, after the completion of the last Kontakion: Let us pray to the Lord.

The choir: Lord, have mercy.

The priest: For holy art Thou, O our God, and unto Thee do we send up glory, to the Father, and to the Son, and to the Holy Spirit, now and ever,

The deacon: and unto the ages of ages.

The choir: Amen.

THE THRICE-HOLY HYMN

HOLY God, Holy Mighty, Holy Immortal, have mercy on us. (3)

Glory to the Father, and to the Son, and to the Holy Spirit;

Both now and ever, and unto the ages of ages. Amen.

Holy Immortal, have mercy on us.

The deacon: Dynamis.

The choir: Dynamis. Holy God, Holy Mighty, Holy Immortal, have mercy on us.

THE READING OF THE EPISTLE

The deacon: Let us attend.

The priest: Peace be unto all.

The choir: And to thy spirit.

The deacon: Wisdom.

The reader then proclaimeth the appointed Prokeimenon, which is chanted in turn by the choir.

The deacon: Wisdom.

The reader proclaimeth the title of the Epistle, and again the deacon: Let us attend.

And the appointed Epistle is read.

After the Epistle, the priest saith: Peace be to thee that readest.

Then the reader proclaimeth the Alleluia *and its verses, and the choir chanteth the* Alleluia *in the appointed tone.*

THE READING OF THE GOSPEL

The priest: Wisdom. Upright. Let us hear the holy Gospel. Peace be unto all.

The choir: And to thy spirit.

The deacon: The reading is from the holy Gospel according to Saint (*Name*).

The choir: Glory to Thee, O Lord, glory to Thee.

The priest: Let us attend.

And the deacon readeth the appointed Gospel.

After the Gospel, the priest saith: Peace be to thee that proclaimest the Gospel.

The choir: Glory to Thee, O Lord, glory to Thee.

THE LITANY OF FERVENT SUPPLICATION

The deacon: Let us all say with our whole soul and with our whole mind, let us say:

> *The choir, after each petition:*
> Lord, have mercy. (3)

The deacon: O Lord Almighty, the God of our Fathers, we pray Thee, hearken and have mercy.

Have mercy on us, O God, according to Thy great mercy, we pray Thee, hearken and have mercy.

Again we pray for pious and Orthodox Christians.

Again we pray for our Bishop (*Name*).

Again we pray for our brethren, priests, priestmonks, deacons, hierodeacons, monks, nuns, and all our brotherhood in Christ.

Again we pray for mercy, life, peace, health, salvation, visitation, pardon and remission of the sins of all pious and Orthodox Christians, the founders, donors, and benefactors of this holy temple, and for the servants of God: (*and he remembereth whom he will of the living*).

Again we pray for the blessed and ever-memorable founders of this holy temple, and for all our fathers and brethren gone to their rest before us, the Orthodox here and everywhere piously laid to rest, and for the servants of God: *(and he remembereth whom he will of the reposed).*

Again we pray for them that bear fruit and do good works in this holy and all-venerable temple; for them that labour and them that chant, and for all the people here present that await Thy great and abundant mercy.

The choir: Lord, have mercy.

The priest: For a merciful and man-befriending God art Thou, and unto Thee do we send up glory, to the Father, and to the Son, and to the Holy Spirit, now and ever, and unto the ages of ages.

The choir: Amen.

THE LITANY OF THE CATECHUMENS

The deacon: Pray, ye catechumens, to the Lord.

The choir, after each petition: Lord, have mercy.

The deacon: Ye faithful, for the catechumens let us pray.

That the Lord may have mercy on them.

That He may catechize them with the word of truth.

That He may reveal unto them the Gospel of righteousness.

That He may unite them to His Holy, Catholic, and Apostolic Church.

Save them, have mercy on them, help them, and keep them, O God, by Thy grace.

The choir: Amen.

The deacon: Ye catechumens, bow your heads unto the Lord.

The choir: To Thee, O Lord.

The priest: That they also with us may glorify Thine all-honourable and majestical Name, of the Father, and of the Son, and of the Holy Spirit, now and ever, and unto the ages of ages.

The choir: Amen.

The deacon: As many as are catechumens, depart. Catechumens depart. As many as are catechumens, depart. Let none of the catechumens remain.

THE FIRST LITANY OF THE FAITHFUL

The deacon: As many as are of the faithful: again and again in peace let us pray to the Lord.

The choir: Lord, have mercy.

The deacon: Help us, save us, have mercy on us, and keep us, O God, by Thy grace.

The choir: Amen.

The deacon: Wisdom.

The priest: For unto Thee is due all glory, honour, and worship, to the Father, and to the Son, and to the Holy Spirit, now and ever, and unto the ages of ages.

The choir: Amen.

THE SECOND LITANY OF THE FAITHFUL

The deacon: Again and again, in peace let us pray to the Lord.

The choir: Lord, have mercy.

The deacon: Help us, save us, have mercy on us, and keep us, O God, by Thy grace.

The choir: Amen.

The deacon: Wisdom.

The priest: That being guarded always under Thy dominion, we may send up glory unto Thee, to the Father, and to the Son, and to the Holy Spirit, now and ever, and unto the ages of ages.

The choir: Amen.

THE GREAT ENTRANCE
THE CHERUBIC HYMN

LET us who mystically portray the Cherubim, and chant the thrice-holy hymn unto the life-creating Trinity, lay aside all earthly care;

At the Great Entrance:

The deacon: All of us, and all pious and Orthodox Christians, may the Lord God remember in His Kingdom, always, now and ever, and unto the ages of ages.

The choir: Amen.

The priest: All of us, and all pious and Orthodox Christians, may the Lord God remember in His Kingdom, always, now and ever, and unto the ages of ages.

The choir: Amen.

The choir completeth the Cherubic Hymn:

THAT we may receive the King of all, escorted invisibly by the angelic orders.
 Alleluia. Alleluia. Alleluia.

THE LITANY OF OBLATION

The deacon: Let us complete our prayer unto the Lord.

The choir, after each petition: Lord, have mercy.

The deacon: For the precious Gifts set forth, let us pray to the Lord.

For this holy house, and them that with faith, reverence, and fear of God enter herein, let us pray to the Lord.

For our deliverance from all tribulation,

wrath, danger, and necessity, let us pray to the Lord.

Help us, save us, have mercy on us, and keep us, O God, by Thy grace.

The choir: Amen.

The deacon: That the whole day may be perfect, holy, peaceful, and sinless, let us ask of the Lord.

The choir, after each petition: Grant this, O Lord.

The deacon: An angel of peace, a faithful guide, a guardian of our souls and bodies, let us ask of the Lord.

Pardon and remission of our sins and offences, let us ask of the Lord.

Things good and profitable for our souls, and peace for the world, let us ask of the Lord.

That we may complete the remaining time of our life in peace and repentance, let us ask of the Lord.

A Christian ending to our life, painless, blameless, peaceful, and a good defence before the dread judgment seat of Christ, let us ask of the Lord.

Calling to remembrance our all-holy, immaculate, most blessed, glorious Lady Theotokos and Ever-virgin Mary with all the Saints, let us commit ourselves and one another and all our life unto Christ our God.

The choir: To Thee, O Lord.

The priest: Through the compassions of Thine Only-begotten Son, with Whom Thou art blessed, together with Thine All-holy and good and life-creating Spirit, now and ever, and unto the ages of ages.

The choir: Amen.

The priest: Peace be unto all.

The choir: And to thy spirit.

The deacon: Let us love one another, that with one mind we may confess:

The choir: Father, Son, and Holy Spirit, the Trinity one in essence and undivided.

But if there is a concelebration, the choir chanteth instead:

I will love Thee, O Lord, my strength; the Lord is my foundation, and my refuge, and my deliverer.

The deacon: The doors! The doors! In wisdom let us attend.

THE SYMBOL OF FAITH

I BELIEVE in one God, the Father Almighty, Maker of heaven and earth, and of all things visible and invisible;

And in one Lord Jesus Christ, the Son of God, the Only-begotten, begotten of the Father before all ages; Light of Light, true God of true God; begotten, not made; being of one essence with the Father; by Whom all things were made;

Who for us men, and for our salvation, came down from the Heavens, and was incarnate of the Holy Spirit and the Virgin Mary, and became man;

And was crucified for us under Pontius Pilate, suffered and was buried;

And arose again on the third day according to the Scriptures;

And ascended into the Heavens, and sitteth at the right hand of the Father;

And shall come again, with glory, to judge both the living and the dead; Whose Kingdom shall have no end;

And in the Holy Spirit, the Lord, the Giver of life; Who proceedeth from the Father; Who with the Father and the Son together is worshipped and glorified; Who spake by the Prophets;

In One, Holy, Catholic, and Apostolic Church.

I confess one baptism for the remission of sins.

I look for the resurrection of the dead,
And the life of the age to come. Amen.

123

THE ANAPHORA

The deacon: Let us stand well. Let us stand with fear. Let us attend, that we may offer the holy oblation in peace.

The choir: A mercy of peace, a sacrifice of praise.

The priest: The grace of our Lord Jesus Christ, and the love of God the Father, and the communion of the Holy Spirit be with you all.

The choir: And with thy spirit.

The priest: Let us lift up our hearts.

The choir: We lift them to the Lord.

The priest: Let us give thanks unto the Lord.

The choir: Meet and right it is to worship Father, Son, and Holy Spirit, the Trinity one in essence and undivided.

The priest: Singing the triumphal hymn, shouting, crying, and saying:

The choir: Holy, Holy, Holy, Lord of Sabaoth, heaven and earth are full of Thy glory. Hosanna in the highest: Blessed is He that cometh in the Name of the Lord. Hosanna in the highest.

The priest, at the Liturgy of Saint John Chrysostom: Take, eat: This is My Body, which is broken for you, for the remission of sins.

But at the Liturgy of Saint Basil, the priest saith: He gave to His holy Disciples and Apostles, saying, Take, eat: This is My Body, which is broken for you, for the remission of sins.

The choir: **Amen.**

The priest, at the Liturgy of Saint John Chrysostom: **Drink ye all of it: This is My Blood of the new testament, which is shed for you and for many, for the remission of sins.**

But at the Liturgy of Saint Basil, the priest saith: He gave to His holy Disciples and Apostles, saying, Drink ye all of it: This is My Blood of the new testament, which is shed for you and for many, for the remission of sins.

The choir: **Amen.**

The priest: **Thine own of Thine own do we offer unto Thee, because of all and for all.**

The choir: **We hymn Thee, we bless Thee, we give thanks to Thee, O Lord, and we entreat Thee, O our God.**

The priest: **Especially our all-holy, immaculate, most blessed, glorious Lady Theotokos and Ever-virgin Mary.**

Then the choir chanteth the following, unless it be a Feast of the Master or of the Mother of God, at which time the appointed Megalynarion is chanted instead.

IT is truly meet to call thee blest, the Theotokos, the ever-blessed and all-immaculate and Mother of our God. More honourable than the Cherubim, and beyond compare more glorious than the Seraphim, thee who without corruption gavest birth to God the Word, the very Theotokos, thee do we magnify.

But at the Liturgy of Saint Basil the Great, if no other Megalynarion is appointed, the following is chanted:

IN thee, O Full of Grace, all creation—both the company of angels and the race of men—doth rejoice. O hallowed temple and spiritual paradise, boast of virgins: from thee God was incarnate, and became a child, He, our God Who existed before the ages; for He made thy womb a throne, and He made thee more spacious than the heavens. In thee, O Full of Grace, all creation doth rejoice. Glory be to thee.

The priest: Among the first, remember, O Lord, our Bishop (*Name*), whom do Thou grant unto Thy holy churches in peace, safety, honour, health, length of days, and rightly dividing the word of Thy truth.

The deacon: And all whom each hath in mind, each and every one.

The choir: Each and every pious and Orthodox Christian.

The Megalynaria of the Saints of the day, or of the Feast being celebrated, may be chanted here.

The priest: And grant us with one mouth and

one heart to glorify and hymn Thine all-honourable and majestical Name, of the Father, and of the Son, and of the Holy Spirit, now and ever, and unto the ages of ages.

The choir: Amen.

The priest: And the mercies of our great God and Saviour Jesus Christ shall be with you all.

The choir: And with thy spirit.

THE LITANY OF SUPPLICATION

The deacon: Calling to remembrance all the Saints, again and again, in peace let us pray to the Lord.

The choir, after each petition: Lord, have mercy.

The deacon: For the precious Gifts offered and sanctified, let us pray to the Lord.

That our man-befriending God, Who hath accepted them upon His holy and noetic altar above the Heavens for an odour of spiritual fragrance, will send down upon us in return the divine grace and the gift of the Holy Spirit, let us pray.

For our deliverance from all tribulation, wrath, danger, and necessity, let us pray to the Lord.

Help us, save us, have mercy on us, and keep us, O God, by Thy grace.

The choir: Amen.

The deacon: That the whole day may be perfect, holy, peaceful, and sinless, let us ask of the Lord.

The choir, after each petition: Grant this, O Lord.

The deacon: An angel of peace, a faithful guide, a guardian of our souls and bodies, let us ask of the Lord.

Pardon and remission of our sins and offences, let us ask of the Lord.

Things good and profitable for our souls, and peace for the world, let us ask of the Lord.

That we may complete the remaining time of our life in peace and repentance, let us ask of the Lord.

A Christian ending to our life, painless, blameless, peaceful, and a good defence before the dread judgment seat of Christ, let us ask of the Lord.

Having asked for the unity of the Faith and the communion of the Holy Spirit, let us commit ourselves and one another and all our life unto Christ our God.

The choir: To Thee, O Lord.

The priest: And account us worthy, O Sovereign Master, that with boldness and without condemnation we may dare to call upon Thee, the Heavenly God, as Father, and to say:

THE LORD'S PRAYER

OUR Father, Which art in the Heavens, hallowed be Thy Name. Thy Kingdom come. Thy will be done, on earth as it is in Heaven. Give us this day our daily bread. And forgive us our debts, as we forgive our debtors. And lead us not into temptation, but deliver us from the evil one.

The priest: For Thine is the kingdom, and the power, and the glory, of the Father, and of the Son, and of the Holy Spirit, now and ever, and unto the ages of ages.

The choir: Amen.

The priest: Peace be unto all.

The choir: And to thy spirit.

The deacon: Bow your heads unto the Lord.

The choir: To Thee, O Lord.

The priest: By the grace and compassions and love for man of Thine Only-begotten Son, with Whom Thou art blessed, together with Thine All-holy and good and life-creating Spirit, now and ever, and unto the ages of ages.

The choir: Amen.

THE ELEVATION

The deacon: Let us attend.

The priest: The Holies for the holy.

The choir: One is holy, One is Lord, Jesus Christ, to the glory of God the Father. Amen.

And the choir chanteth the appointed Communion Hymn.

THE COMMUNION OF THE FAITHFUL

The deacon: With fear of God, faith, and love, draw near.

The choir: Blessed is He that cometh in the Name of the Lord. God is the Lord, and hath appeared unto us.

The priest: I believe, O Lord, and I confess that Thou art truly the Christ, the Son of the Living God, Who camest into the world to save sinners, of whom I am chief. Furthermore, I believe that This is indeed Thine immaculate Body, and that This is indeed Thy precious Blood. Wherefore, I pray Thee: Have mercy on me and forgive me my transgressions, voluntary and involuntary, in word and deed, in knowledge and in ignorance. And vouchsafe that, uncondemned, I may partake of Thine immaculate Mysteries unto the remission of sins and unto life everlasting. Amen.

Of Thy Mystic Supper, O Son of God, receive me today as a communicant; for I will not speak of the Mystery to Thine enemies; nor will I give Thee a kiss as did Judas; but like the thief do I confess Thee: Remember me, O Lord, in Thy Kingdom. Remember me, O Master, in Thy Kingdom. Remember me, O Holy One, in Thy Kingdom.

The priest imparteth of the Holy Mysteries to the communicants.

The choir chanteth: Of Thy Mystic Supper . . . , Partake ye of the Body of Christ . . . , *and such like hymns, according to the number of communicants.*

Following the communion of the faithful, the priest blesseth the people, saying: Save, O God, Thy people, and bless Thine inheritance.

The choir: We have seen the true Light. We have received the Heavenly Spirit. We have found the true Faith, in worshipping the indivisible Trinity; for He hath saved us.

The priest: Always, now and ever, and unto the ages of ages.

The choir: Amen. Let our mouth be filled with Thy praise, O Lord, that we may hymn Thy glory; for Thou hast counted us worthy to partake of Thy holy Mysteries; preserve us in Thy sanctification, meditating on Thy righteousness all the day long. Alleluia.

THE LITANY OF THANKSGIVING

The deacon: Upright. Having partaken of the divine, holy, immaculate, immortal, heavenly and life-creating, fearful Mysteries of Christ, let us worthily give thanks unto the Lord.

The choir: Glory to Thee, O Lord, glory to Thee.

The deacon: Help us, save us, have mercy on us, and keep us, O God, by Thy grace.

The choir: Amen.

The deacon: Having asked that the whole day may be perfect, holy, peaceful, and sinless, let us commit ourselves and one another and all our life unto Christ our God.

The choir: To Thee, O Lord.

The priest: For Thou art our sanctification, and unto Thee do we send up glory, to the Father, and to the Son, and to the Holy Spirit, now and ever, and unto the ages of ages.

The choir: Amen.

The priest: In peace let us depart.

The choir: In the Name of the Lord.

The deacon: Let us pray to the Lord.

The choir: Lord, have mercy.

THE PRAYER BEHIND THE AMBO
FOR THE LITURGY OF
SAINT JOHN CHRYSOSTOM

The priest:

O LORD, Who blessest them that bless Thee, and sanctifiest them that put their trust in Thee: save Thy people, and bless Thine inheritance. Preserve the fulness of Thy Church, sanctify them that love the beauty of Thy house. Do Thou in turn glorify them by Thy divine power, and forsake us not that hope in Thee. Give peace to Thy world, to Thy churches, to the priests, to those in authority, and to all Thy people. For every good giving and every perfect gift is from above and cometh down from Thee, the Father of lights, and unto Thee do we send up glory, thanksgiving, and worship, to the Father, and to the Son, and to the Holy Spirit, now and ever, and unto the ages of ages.

But if the Liturgy of Saint Basil the Great hath been celebrated, the priest saith:

THE PRAYER BEHIND THE AMBO
FOR THE LITURGY OF
SAINT BASIL THE GREAT

O CHRIST our God, Who for a sacrifice of praise and a well-pleasing worship acceptest this rational and unbloody sacrifice from them that with their whole heart call upon Thee, the Lamb and Son of God which takest away the sin of the world, the blameless Calf which receivest not the yoke of sin and wast sacrificed for us willingly; which art broken, yet not severed, which art eaten, yet never consumed, but sanctifying those who partake thereof; Who in remembrance of Thy voluntary Passion and Thy life-giving Arising on the third day hast made us communicants of Thine ineffable and heavenly and dread Mysteries, even Thy holy Body and Thy precious Blood: keep us Thy servants, the ministers and the people here present, in Thy sanctification; and grant us at every time and season to meditate on Thy righteousness, that being led according to Thy will, and doing the things that well-please Thee, we also may become worthy of a place at Thy right hand, when Thou shalt come to judge the living and the dead. Rescue our brethren in captivity; visit those in sickness; pilot those in perils at sea; and give repose where the light of Thy countenance shineth to the souls that have gone to their rest in the hope of everlasting life; and hearken to all who beseech Thine aid. For Thou art the Giver of every good, and we send up glory to Thee, with Thy Father which is without beginning, and Thine All-holy and good and life-creating Spirit, now, and ever, and unto the ages of ages.

The choir: Amen. Blessed be the Name of the Lord, from henceforth and forevermore. (3)

The deacon: Let us pray to the Lord.

The choir: Lord, have mercy.

The priest: The blessing of the Lord and His mercy come upon you, by His divine grace and love for man, always, now and ever, and unto the ages of ages.

The choir: Amen.

The priest: Glory to Thee, O God, our hope, glory to Thee.

The choir: Glory to the Father, and to the Son, and to the Holy Spirit; both now and ever, and unto the ages of ages. Amen.
Lord, have mercy (3). Holy Father, bless.

The priest:

HE that arose from the dead (*if it be the Lord's Day; or if it be a Feast of the Master, the appointed dismissal; but if not, then he beginneth:*) Christ our true God, by the intercessions of His all-immaculate and all-blameless holy Mother, by the power of the honoured and life-giving Cross, by the protection of the venerable, heavenly Bodiless Powers, by the supplications of the venerable, glorious Prophet, Forerunner, and Baptist John, of the holy, glorious, and all-famed Apostles, of the holy, glorious, victorious

Martyrs, of our righteous and God-bearing Fathers, of (*the Saint to whom the temple is dedicated*), of the holy, righteous Ancestors of God Joachim and Anna, of (*the Saints of the day*), whose memory we celebrate, and of our Father among the Saints, John Chrysostom, Archbishop of Constantinople, (*or* our Father among the Saints, Basil the Great, Archbishop of Caesarea in Cappadocia) whose Liturgy we have celebrated, and of all the Saints—may He have mercy on us and save us, for He is good and the Friend of man.

Through the prayers of our holy Fathers, Lord Jesus Christ our God, have mercy on us.

The choir: **Amen.**

Then the priest distributeth the antidoron to the faithful who have not partaken of Communion, and the Prayers of Thanksgiving after Holy Communion are read (see page 373).

DISMISSAL HYMNS OF
THE RESURRECTION

In the Eight Tones with Their
Theotokia and Kontakia

FIRST TONE
Dismissal Hymn

WHEN the stone had been sealed by the Jews and the soldiers were guarding Thine immaculate Body, Thou didst arise on the third day, O Saviour, granting life unto the world. Wherefore, the powers of the Heavens cried out to Thee, O Life-giver: Glory to Thy Resurrection, O Christ. Glory to Thy Kingdom. Glory to Thy dispensation, O only Friend of man.

Theotokion. The Original Melody

WHILE Gabriel was saying Rejoice to thee, O Virgin, at his voice the Master of all things took flesh within thy pure womb. He dwelt in thee as His holy ark as spake the righteous David in the psalms. And in bearing thy

Creator, thou wast shown forth more spacious than all the Heavens. Glory to Him that willed to dwell in thee. Glory to Him that came forth from thee. Glory to Him that, through thy bringing forth, hath delivered us.

Kontakion

As God, Thou didst arise from the tomb in glory, and Thou didst raise the world together with Thyself. And mortal nature praised Thee as God, and death was obliterated. And Adam danceth for joy, O Master, and Eve, now freed from fetters, rejoiceth as she crieth out: Thou, O Christ, dost grant resurrection unto all.

SECOND TONE
Dismissal Hymn

When Thou didst descend unto death, O Life Immortal, then didst Thou slay Hades with the lightning of Thy Divinity. And when Thou didst also raise the dead out of the nethermost depths, all the powers in the Heavens cried out: O Life-giver, Christ our God, glory be to Thee.

Theotokion

All thy mysteries are beyond comprehension; all are exceedingly glorious, O Theotokos. Sealed with purity and preserved in virginity, thou wast known to be a true mother, giving birth unto the true God. Do thou entreat Him that our souls be saved.

Kontakion. Thou soughtest the heights

A RISEN art Thou, Almighty Saviour, from the tomb; as Hades beheld, he trembled at the miracle; and the dead arose, and creation, seeing this, doth rejoice with Thee; and as Adam also is glad, the world, O my Saviour, praiseth Thee for ever.

THIRD TONE
Dismissal Hymn

L ET the Heavens rejoice; let earthly things be glad; for the Lord hath wrought might with His arm, He hath trampled upon death by death. The first-born of the dead hath He become. From the belly of Hades hath He delivered us, and hath granted great mercy to the world.

Theotokion

W E praise thee, the Mediatress for the salvation of our race, O Virgin Theotokos; for in the flesh taken from thee, thy Son and our God hath deigned to endure the Passion through the Cross, and hath redeemed us from corruption, since He is the Friend of man.

Kontakion. On this day the Virgin

O N this day didst Thou arise out of the grave and didst lead us from the bars and gates of death, Thou Who art great in compassion. On this day, both Adam danceth and Eve rejoiceth; and with them, all of the Patriarchs and the Prophets chant unceasing hymns in praise of the godly power of Thy dominion and might.

FOURTH TONE
Dismissal Hymn

HAVING learned the joyful proclamation of the Resurrection from the Angel, and having cast off the ancestral condemnation, the women disciples of the Lord spake to the Apostles exultantly: Death is despoiled and Christ God is risen, granting great mercy to the world.

Theotokion

THE mystery hidden from eternity and unknown to the Angels is made manifest through thee, O Theotokos, to those on earth. God became incarnate in an unmingled union and for our sake hath submitted willingly to the Cross, whereby He hath raised up the firstfashioned man and hath saved our souls from death.

Kontakion. On this day Thou hast appeared

NOW hath my Deliverer and mighty Saviour raised the earthborn from the grave and from their bonds, since He is God; and He hath crushed Hades' brazen gates and is arisen the third day as Sovereign Lord.

Dismissal Hymn. The Original Melody

LET us worship the Word, O ye faithful, praising Him that with the Father and Spirit is co-beginningless God, Who was born of a pure Virgin that we all be saved; for He was pleased to mount the Cross in the flesh that He assumed, accepting thus to endure death. And by His glorious rising, He also willed to resurrect the dead.

Theotokion. Same Melody

O IMPASSABLE gate of the Lord Most High, rejoice. Rejoice, O rampart and shelter for them that hasten to thee. Tranquil haven and pure Maiden who didst not know man and who didst give birth in the flesh to thy Maker and thy God, rejoice; and cease not to pray Him, making entreaty for them that worship and praise Him that was born of thee.

Kontakion

IN Thy condescension, Thou didst descend into Hades, O my Saviour, and having broken the gates since Thou art omnipotent, as Creator Thou didst raise up the dead together with Thyself. And Thou didst break the sting of death, O

Christ, and didst deliver Adam from the curse, O Friend of man. Wherefore, we all cry unto Thee: Save us, O Lord.

PLAGAL OF SECOND TONE
Dismissal Hymn

ANGELIC powers were above Thy tomb, and they that guarded Thee became as dead. And Mary stood by the grave seeking Thine immaculate Body. Thou hast despoiled Hades and wast not tried thereby. Thou didst meet the Virgin and didst grant us life. O Thou Who didst arise from the dead, Lord, glory be to Thee.

Theotokion

THOU Who didst call Thy mother blessed, camest of Thine own free will unto the Passion, shining forth upon the Cross, wishing to seek out Adam, and saying unto the Angels: Rejoice with Me, for the drachma that was lost is found. Thou Who hast wisely governed all things, glory be to Thee.

Kontakion

HAVING raised up all the dead out of the dark abysses by His life-bestowing hand, Christ God, the Giver of Life, hath bestowed the Resurrection upon mortal nature; for He is the Saviour and Resurrection and Life of all, and the God of all.

GRAVE TONE
Dismissal Hymn

THOU didst abolish death by Thy Cross; Thou didst open Paradise to the thief; Thou didst transform the myrrh-bearers' lamentation, and didst bid Thine Apostles to preach that Thou art risen, O Christ God, granting great mercy to the world.

Theotokion

As the treasury of our resurrection, O all-hymned one, do thou lead forth from the pit and abyss of offences them that hope in thee; for those that were guilty because of sin hast thou saved by giving birth to Salvation, O thou who before childbirth wast virgin, and in childbirth wast virgin, and after childbirth again remainest virgin.

Kontakion

No longer will the dominion of death be able to keep men captive; for Christ hath descended, destroying and dispelling the powers thereof. Hades is bound; the Prophets rejoice with one accord, saying: A Saviour hath come for them that have faith. Come forth, ye faithful, for the Resurrection.

PLAGAL OF FOURTH TONE
Dismissal Hymn

FROM on high didst Thou descend, O Compassionate One; to burial of three days hast Thou submitted that Thou mightest free us from our passions. O our Life and Resurrection, Lord, glory be to Thee.

Theotokion

O THOU Who for our sakes wast born of a Virgin, and didst suffer crucifixion, O Good One, and didst despoil death by death, and as God, didst reveal the Resurrection: Disdain them not which Thou hast fashioned with Thy hand; show us Thy love for mankind, O Merciful One; accept the Theotokos that gave Thee birth, who intercedeth for us; and do Thou, our Saviour, save a despairing people.

Kontakion. As first-fruits of our nature

ARISING from the tomb, O mighty Saviour, Thou didst rouse the dead; Thou didst raise Adam; while Eve danceth in her joy at Thy blest Resurrection, O Lord. And the world's farthest regions keep the festival on Thine arising from the dead with gladness and thanksgiving, O Thou Who art greatly merciful.

DISMISSAL HYMNS AND
THEOTOKIA FOR
WEEKDAYS

Chanted When There is No Feast

FOR SUNDAY VESPERS
AND MONDAY MORNING
Fourth Tone. Thou Who wast raised up

SUPREME Commanders of the Hosts of the Heavens, we, the unworthy, importune and beseech you that by your supplications ye encircle us in the shelter of the wings of your immaterial glory, guarding us who now fall down and cry to you with fervour: Deliver us from dangers of all kinds, as the great marshals of the heavenly hosts on high.

Theotokion

UNTO her that was reared in the Temple, in the Holy of Holies, and who was adorned with faith and wisdom and blameless virginity, did the Supreme Commander Gabriel bring the salutation from Heaven and the greeting: Rejoice. Rejoice, O blessed one. Rejoice, thou who art glorified; the Lord is with thee.

FOR MONDAY VESPERS
AND TUESDAY MORNING
Second Tone

THE memory of the just is celebrated with hymns of praise, but the Lord's testimony is sufficient for thee, O Forerunner; for thou hast proved to be truly even more venerable than the Prophets since thou wast granted to baptize in the running waters Him Whom they proclaimed. Wherefore, having contested for the truth, thou didst rejoice to announce the good tidings even to those in Hades: that God hath appeared in the flesh, taking away the sin of the world and granting us great mercy.

Theotokion

WE have become partakers of the Divine nature through thee, O ever-virgin Theotokos; for thou hast borne the Incarnate God for us. Wherefore, as is due, we all magnify thee reverently.

FOR TUESDAY VESPERS
AND WEDNESDAY MORNING
First Tone

SAVE, O Lord, Thy people, and bless Thine inheritance; grant Thou unto the faithful victory over adversaries. And by the power of Thy Cross do Thou preserve Thy commonwealth.

Theotokion

HAVING thy protection, O immaculate one, and being delivered from afflictions by thy prayers, we who are in every way guarded by the Cross of thy Son do all magnify thee reverently as is due.

FOR WEDNESDAY VESPERS
AND THURSDAY MORNING
Third Tone

O HOLY Apostles, intercede with the merciful God that He grant unto our souls forgiveness of offences.

Fourth Tone   *Nicholas*

THE truth of things hath revealed thee to thy flock as a rule of faith, an icon of meekness, and a teacher of temperance; for this cause thou hast achieved the heights by humility, riches by poverty. O Father and Hierarch Nicholas, intercede with Christ God that our souls be saved.

Theotokion

WE know the Word of the Father, even Christ our God, to be incarnate of thee,

147

O Virgin Theotokos, O only pure one, O only blessed one. Wherefore, we magnify thee, praising thee unceasingly.

FOR THURSDAY VESPERS
AND FRIDAY MORNING
First Tone

SAVE, O Lord, Thy people, and bless Thine inheritance; grant Thou unto the faithful victory over adversaries. And by the power of Thy Cross do Thou preserve Thy commonwealth.

Theotokion

HAVING thy protection, O immaculate one, and being delivered from afflictions by thy prayers, we who are in every way guarded by the Cross of thy Son do all magnify thee reverently as is due.

FOR FRIDAY VESPERS
AND SATURDAY MORNING
Second Tone

O APOSTLES, martyrs, prophets, hierarchs, righteous, and just ones, who have finished your course well and have kept the Faith: seeing ye have boldness with the Saviour, beseech Him for us, since He is good, that our souls be saved, we pray.

Glory.
For the Reposed. Plagal of Fourth Tone

KEEP Thy servants in remembrance, O Lord, since Thou art good, and do Thou forgive their every sin in this life; for no man is without sin, except for Thee Who art able to grant rest even unto those that have departed hence.

Both now. *Theotokion*

O HOLY Mother of the Ineffable Light, with reverence we magnify thee, honouring thee with angelic hymns.

149

Ή ΜΕΤΑΜόΡφωcιc

THE TRANSFIGURATION

DISMISSAL HYMNS
AND KONTAKIA OF THE
FEASTS OF THE MASTER
AND OF THE
MOTHER OF GOD

The Nativity of Our Most Holy Lady,
the Theotokos and Ever-virgin Mary
Dismissal Hymn. Fourth Tone

THY Nativity, O Theotokos, hath proclaimed joy to the whole world; for from thee hath dawned the Sun of Righteousness, Christ our God, annulling the curse and bestowing the blessing, abolishing death and granting us life everlasting.

Kontakion. Fourth Tone

JOACHIM and Anna were freed from the reproach of childlessness, and Adam and Eve from the corruption of death, O immaculate one, by thy holy Nativity, which thy people, redeemed from the guilt of offences, celebrate by crying to thee: The barren woman giveth birth to the Theotokos, the nourisher of our life.

SEPTEMBER 14

The Exaltation of the Precious
and Life-giving Cross

Dismissal Hymn. First Tone

SAVE, O Lord, Thy people and bless Thine inheritance; grant Thou unto the faithful victory over adversaries. And by the power of Thy Cross do Thou preserve Thy commonwealth.

Kontakion. Fourth Tone. The Original Melody

THOU Who wast raised up on the Cross of Thine own will, O Christ our God, do Thou bestow Thy compassions upon this, Thy new commonwealth named after Thee. Gladden with Thy sovereign might our most Orthodox hierarchs, and vouchsafe them victory over every false teaching; and as Thy help in war may they possess the weapon of peace, the trophy invincible.

NOVEMBER 21

The Entry into the Temple of Our Most Holy Lady,
the Theotokos and Ever-virgin Mary

Dismissal Hymn. Fourth Tone

TODAY is the prelude of God's good will and the heralding of the salvation of mankind. In the temple of God, the Virgin is presented openly, and she proclaimeth Christ unto all. To her, then, with a great voice let us cry aloud: Rejoice, O thou fulfilment of the Creator's dispensation.

Kontakion. Fourth Tone. Thou Who wast raised up

THE sacred treasury of God's holy glory, the greatly precious bridal chamber and Virgin, the Saviour's most pure temple, free of stain and undefiled, into the House of the Lord on this day is brought forward and bringeth with herself the grace of the Most Divine Spirit; her do God's Angels hymn with songs of praise, for she is truly the heavenly tabernacle.

DECEMBER 25
The Nativity of Our Lord and God
and Saviour Jesus Christ
Dismissal Hymn. Fourth Tone

THY Nativity, O Christ our God, hath shined the light of knowledge upon the world; for thereby they that worshipped the stars were instructed by a star to worship Thee, the Sun of Righteousness, and to know Thee, the Dayspring from on high. O Lord, glory be to Thee.

Kontakion. Third Tone. The Original Melody

ON this day the Virgin beareth the Transcendent in essence; to the Unapproachable, the earth doth offer a small cave; Angels join in choir with shepherds in giving glory;

with a star the Magi travel upon their journey;
for our sakes is born a young Child, He that
existed before the ages as God.

JANUARY 6

The Holy Theophany (Epiphany) of Our Lord,
and God, and Saviour Jesus Christ

Dismissal Hymn. First Tone

WHEN Thou wast baptized in the Jordan,
O Lord, the worship of the Trinity was
made manifest; for the voice of the Father bare
witness to Thee, calling Thee His beloved Son.
And the Spirit in the form of a dove confirmed
the certainty of the word. O Christ our God,
Who hast appeared and hast enlightened the
world, glory be to Thee.

Kontakion. Fourth Tone. The Original Melody

ON this day Thou hast appeared unto the
whole world, and Thy light, O Sovereign
Lord, is signed on us who sing Thy praise and
chant with knowledge: Thou hast now come,
Thou hast appeared, O Thou Light unapproachable.

FEBRUARY 2

The Meeting of Our Lord, and God, and Saviour
Jesus Christ in the Temple

Dismissal Hymn. First Tone

REJOICE, thou who art full of grace, O Virgin Theotokos, for from thee hath risen

the Sun of Righteousness, Christ our God, enlightening those in darkness. Rejoice, thou also, O righteous Elder, as thou receivest in thine arms the Redeemer of our souls, Who also granteth unto us the Resurrection.

Kontakion. First Tone

THOU Who didst sanctify the Virgin's womb by Thy birth, and didst bless Symeon's hands as was meet, by anticipation hast even now saved us, O Christ God. But grant peace in the midst of wars unto Thy commonwealth and strengthen the hierarchs whom Thou hast loved, O only Friend of man.

MARCH 25
The Annunciation of Our Most Holy Lady, the Theotokos and Ever-virgin Mary
Dismissal Hymn. Fourth Tone

TODAY is the fountainhead of our salvation and the manifestation of the mystery which was from eternity. The Son of God becometh the Virgin's Son, and Gabriel announceth the good tidings of grace; for this cause, let us cry to the Mother of God with him: Rejoice, thou who art full of grace, the Lord is with thee.

Kontakion. Plagal of Fourth Tone
The Original Melody

WHEN the bodiless one learned the secret command, in haste he came and stood before Joseph's dwelling, and spake unto the Maiden who knew not wedlock: The One Who hath bowed the Heavens by His descent is held and contained unchanging wholly in thee. Seeing Him receiving the form of a servant in thy womb, I stand in awe and cry to thee:

Rejoice, thou Bride unwedded.

Another Kontakion. Plagal of Fourth Tone
The Original Melody

To thee, the Champion Leader, we thy flock dedicate a feast of victory and of thanksgiving as ones rescued out of sufferings, O Theotokos; but as thou art one with might which is invincible, from all dangers that can be do thou deliver us, that we may cry to thee:

Rejoice, thou Bride unwedded.

AUGUST 6

The Transfiguration of Our Lord, and God,
and Saviour, Jesus Christ
Dismissal Hymn. Grave Tone

THOU wast transfigured on the mountain, O Christ our God, showing to Thy disciples Thy glory as each one could endure. Shine forth Thou on us, who are sinners all, Thy light ever-unending, through the prayers of the Theotokos. Light-bestower, glory to Thee.

Kontakion. Grave Tone

ON the mount Thou wast transfigured, and Thy disciples, as much as they could bear, beheld Thy glory, O Christ our God; that when they should see Thee crucified, they would know Thy Passion to be willing, and would preach to the world that Thou, in truth, art the Effulgence of the Father.

AUGUST 15

The Dormition of Our Most Holy Lady, the Theotokos and Ever-virgin Mary

Dismissal Hymn. First Tone

IN giving birth, thou didst preserve thy virginity; in thy dormition, thou didst not forsake the world, O Theotokos. Thou wast translated unto life, since thou art the Mother of Life; and by thine intercessions dost thou redeem our souls from death.

Kontakion. Second Tone

THE grave and death could not hold the Theotokos, who is unsleeping in her intercessions and an unfailing hope in her mediations. For as the Mother of Life she was translated to life by Him Who dwelt in her ever-virgin womb.

DISMISSAL HYMNS AND KONTAKIA OF **THE TRIODION**

SUNDAY OF THE PUBLICAN AND PHARISEE

Kontakion. Fourth Tone
On this day Thou hast appeared

LET us flee the Pharisee's conceited vaunting; let us learn the Publican's humility, and cry with groans unto the Saviour: Thou Who alone art swiftly reconciled, be gracious unto us.

SUNDAY OF THE PRODIGAL SON

Kontakion. Third Tone
On this day the Virgin

FOOLISHLY I sprang away from Thy great fatherly glory, and dispersed in wicked deeds the riches that Thou didst give me. With the Prodigal I therefore cry unto Thee now: I have sinned against Thee, O compassionate Father. But receive me in repentance; make me as one of Thy hired servants, O Lord.

SATURDAY OF MEAT-FARE WEEK
Commemoration of All Orthodox
Christians Who have Reposed
Dismissal Hymn. Plagal of Fourth Tone

O THOU Who by the depth of Thy wisdom dost provide all things out of love for man, and grantest unto all that which is profitable, O only Creator: Grant rest, O Lord, to the souls of Thy servants; for in Thee have they placed their hope, O our Creator and Fashioner and God.

Kontakion. Plagal of Fourth Tone

WITH the Saints grant rest, O Christ, to the souls of Thy servants, where there is neither pain, nor sorrow, nor sighing, but life unending.

MEAT-FARE SUNDAY
The Sunday of the Last Judgment
Kontakion. First Tone

WHEN Thou, O God, wilt come to earth with glory, and all things tremble, and the river of fire floweth before the Judgment Seat, and the books are opened and the hidden things made public, then deliver me from the unquenchable fire, and deem me worthy to stand at Thy right hand, O most righteous Judge.

CHEESE-FARE SATURDAY

Commemoration of All Our Righteous and God-bearing
Fathers and Mothers Who Shone Forth
in the Ascetical Life

Dismissal Hymn. Fourth Tone

O GOD of our Fathers, ever dealing with us according to Thy gentleness: take not Thy mercy from us, but by their entreaties guide our life in peace.

Kontakion. Plagal of Fourth Tone
As first-fruits of our nature

A s preachers of true piety who silenced all impiety, Lord, Thou hast made the whole host of God-bearing Saints shine forth with splendour on the world. By their prayers and entreaties, keep all them that extol and sincerely magnify Thee in perfect peace, to chant and to sing to Thee: Alleluia.

CHEESE-FARE SUNDAY

The Sunday of Forgiveness, and the Commemoration
of Adam's Exile from Paradise

Kontakion. Plagal of Second Tone

O THOU Guide unto wisdom, Bestower of prudence, Instructor of the foolish, and Defender of the poor: establish and grant understanding unto my heart, O Master. Grant me speech, O Word of the Father; for behold, I shall not keep my lips from crying unto Thee: Have mercy, O Merciful One, on me who have fallen.

THE DISMISSAL HYMNS OF LENTEN VESPERS
Plagal of First Tone

O THEOTOKOS and Virgin, rejoice, O Mary, full of grace; the Lord is with thee. Blessed art thou among women, and blessed is the Fruit of thy womb; for thou hast borne the Saviour of our souls. (*Prostration*)

O BAPTIST of Christ, keep us all in remembrance, that we may be delivered from our iniquities; for to thee was given grace to intercede in our behalf. (*Prostration*)

Glory.

P LEAD in our behalf, O holy Apostles and all Saints, that we may be delivered from perils and afflictions; for we have you as fervent suppliants before the Saviour. (*Prostration*)

Both now.

U NDER thy compassion do we flee, O Theotokos; disdain not our prayers in times of affliction; but do thou rescue us from perils, O only pure one, O only blessed one.

The Holy and Great Fast beginneth on the Monday following Cheese-fare (Forgiveness) Sunday.

FIRST SATURDAY OF THE FAST
The Commemoration of the Miracle of the Kollyva
wrought by Saint Theodore the Tyro
Dismissal Hymn. Second Tone

G REAT are the achievements of faith! In the
fountain of flame, as by the water of rest,
the holy Martyr Theodore rejoiced; for having
been made a whole-burnt offering in the fire,
he was offered as sweet bread unto the Trinity.
By his prayers, O Christ God, save our souls.

Kontakion. Plagal of Fourth Tone

H AVING received the Faith of Christ in thy
heart as a breastplate, thou didst trample
upon the enemy hosts, O much-suffering
champion; and thou hast been crowned eternally with a heavenly crown, since thou art
invincible.

FIRST SUNDAY OF THE FAST
The Sunday of Orthodoxy
Dismissal Hymn. Second Tone

W E worship Thine immaculate icon, O
Good One, asking the forgiveness of our
failings, O Christ our God; for of Thine own
will Thou wast well-pleased to ascend the Cross
in the flesh, that Thou mightest deliver from
slavery to the enemy those whom Thou hadst
fashioned. Wherefore, we cry to Thee thank-

fully: Thou didst fill all things with joy, O our Saviour, when Thou camest to save the world.

Kontakion. Plagal of Fourth Tone

THE undepictable Word of the Father became depictable when He took flesh of thee, O Theotokos; and when He had restored the defiled image to its ancient state, He suffused it with divine beauty. As for us, confessing our salvation, we record it in deed and word.

SECOND SUNDAY OF THE FAST
Saint Gregory Palamas, Archbishop of Thessalonica
Dismissal Hymn. Plagal of Fourth Tone

LIGHT of Orthodoxy, pillar and teacher of the Church, adornment of monastics, invincible champion of theologians, O Gregory thou wonderworker, boast of Thessalonica, herald of grace: ever pray that our souls be saved.

Kontakion. Plagal of Fourth Tone
To thee, the Champion Leader

WITH one accord, we praise thee as the sacred and divine vessel of wisdom and clear trumpet of theology, O our righteous Father Gregory of divine speech. As a mind that standeth now before the Primal Mind, do thou ever guide aright and lead our mind to Him, that we all may cry: Rejoice, O herald of grace divine.

THIRD SUNDAY OF THE FAST
The Worship of the Precious and Life-giving Cross
Dismissal Hymn. First Tone

SAVE, O Lord, Thy people, and bless Thine inheritance; grant Thou unto the faithful victory over adversaries. And by the power of Thy Cross do Thou preserve Thy commonwealth.

Kontakion. Grave Tone

No longer doth the flaming sword guard the gate of Eden, for a marvellous quenching is come upon it, even the Tree of the Cross. The sting hath been taken from death, and the victory from Hades. And Thou, my Saviour, hast appeared unto those in Hades, saying: Enter ye again into Paradise.

FOURTH SUNDAY OF THE FAST
Saint John of the Ladder
Dismissal Hymn. Third Tone. Thy confession

THOU didst scale the mount of godly virtue, to raise up a great and sacred ladder, on the which we ascend from this fallen state; and leaving passions beneath, we rise step by step unto the vision of God and the life on high. Hence, O righteous Father John, as our God-appointed guide, entreat the Lord to grant great mercy unto us.

Kontakion. First Tone. The soldiers standing guard

As ever-blooming fruits, thou dost offer the teachings of thy God-given book, O wise John, thou most blessed, while sweetening the hearts of all them that heed it with vigilance; for it is a ladder from the earth unto Heaven that conferreth glory on the souls that ascend it and honour thee faithfully.

THURSDAY OF THE FIFTH WEEK
The Great Canon of Saint Andrew of Crete
Kontakion. Plagal of Second Tone

My soul, my soul, arise! Wherefore dost thou slumber? The end is drawing nigh, and thou shalt be troubled. Arouse thyself, therefore, that Christ God may spare thee; for He is everywhere present and filleth all things.

SATURDAY OF THE AKATHIST HYMN
*Dismissal Hymn. Plagal of Fourth Tone
The Original Melody*

When the bodiless one learned the secret command, in haste he came and stood before Joseph's dwelling, and spake unto the Maiden who knew not wedlock: The One Who hath bowed the Heavens by His descent is held and contained unchanging wholly in thee. Seeing Him receiving the form of a servant in thy womb, I stand in awe and cry to thee:

Rejoice, thou Bride unwedded.

Kontakion. Plagal of Fourth Tone
The Original Melody

To thee, the Champion Leader, we thy flock dedicate a feast of victory and of thanksgiving, as ones rescued out of sufferings, O Theotokos; but as thou art one with might which is invincible, from all dangers that can be do thou deliver us, that we may cry to thee:
Rejoice, thou Bride unwedded.

FIFTH SUNDAY OF THE FAST
Saint Mary of Egypt
Dismissal Hymn. Plagal of Fourth Tone

In thee the image was preserved with exactness, O Mother; for taking up thy cross, thou didst follow Christ, and by thy deeds thou didst teach us to overlook the flesh, for it passeth away, but to attend to the soul since it is immortal. Wherefore, O righteous Mary, thy spirit rejoiceth with the Angels.

Kontakion. Third Tone. On this day the Virgin

Thou who once wast wholly filled with every wanton defilement art today shown forth to be a bride of Christ through repentance. Thou didst long to live the godly life of the Angels; with the Cross, thou didst subdue and trample down demons. Wherefore, O all-modest Mary, now in the Kingdom thou art an honourable bride.

LAZARUS SATURDAY
Dismissal Hymn. First Tone

IN confirming the common Resurrection, O Christ God, Thou didst raise up Lazarus from the dead before Thy Passion. Wherefore, we also, like the children, bearing the symbols of victory, cry to Thee, the Vanquisher of death: Hosanna in the highest; blessed is He that cometh in the Name of the Lord.

Kontakion. Second Tone
Thou soughtest the heights

TO those on the earth, the Joy of all, Christ God, the Truth, the Light and the Life, the Resurrection of the world, in His goodness hath now appeared and is become the true archetype of the Resurrection of all, bestowing divine forgiveness on all men.

PALM SUNDAY
The Entry of the Lord into Jerusalem
Dismissal Hymn. First Tone

IN confirming the common Resurrection, O Christ God, Thou didst raise up Lazarus from the dead before Thy Passion. Wherefore, we also, like the children, bearing the symbols of victory, cry to Thee, the Vanquisher of death: Hosanna in the highest; blessed is He that cometh in the Name of the Lord.

Another Dismissal Hymn. Fourth Tone

As by baptism we were buried with Thee, O Christ our God, so by Thy Resurrection we were deemed worthy of immortal life; and praising Thee, we cry: Hosanna in the highest; blessed is He that cometh in the Name of the Lord.

Kontakion. Plagal of Second Tone

Being borne upon a throne in Heaven, and upon a colt on the earth, O Christ God, Thou didst accept the praise of the Angels and the laudation of the children as they cried to Thee: Blessed art Thou Who comest to recall Adam.

EXTREME HUMILITY

DISMISSAL HYMNS
AND KONTAKIA FOR
HOLY WEEK

HOLY AND GREAT MONDAY
Troparion. Plagal of Fourth Tone

Behold, the Bridegroom cometh in the middle of the night, and blessed is that servant whom He shall find watching; and again unworthy is he whom He shall find heedless. Beware, therefore, O my soul, lest thou be borne down with sleep, lest thou be given up to death, and be shut out from the Kingdom. But rather rouse thyself and cry: Holy, Holy, Holy art Thou, O our God; by the protection of the Bodiless Hosts, have mercy on us.

This hymn is chanted thrice: twice as above, but the third time, the ending by the protection ... *is replaced by:* through the Theotokos, have mercy on us.

Kontakion. Plagal of Fourth Tone

Jacob lamented the loss of Joseph, but that noble one was seated in a chariot and honoured as a king; for by not being enslaved then to the pleasures of the Egyptian woman, he was glorified by Him that beholdeth the hearts of men and bestoweth an incorruptible crown.

HOLY AND GREAT TUESDAY
Troparion. Plagal of Fourth Tone

Behold, the Bridegroom cometh in the middle of the night . . . *chanted as above for Monday, with the ending the first two times:* by the intercessions of the Forerunner, have mercy on us.

Kontakion. Second Tone

Being mindful of the hour of the end, O my soul, and fearing because of the cutting down of the fig tree, labour diligently with the talent that was given thee, O hapless one, and be watchful and cry: Let us not remain outside the bridal chamber of Christ.

HOLY AND GREAT WEDNESDAY
Troparion. Plagal of Fourth Tone

Behold, the Bridegroom cometh in the middle of the night . . . *chanted as above for Monday, with the ending the first two times:* by the power of Thy Cross, have mercy on us.

Kontakion. Fourth Tone

THOUGH I have transgressed more than the harlot, O Good One, I have in no wise brought forth streams of tears for Thee; but in silence, I supplicate Thee and fall down before Thee, kissing Thine immaculate feet with love, so that, as Master that Thou art, Thou mayest grant me the forgiveness of debts, as I cry to Thee, O Saviour: From the mire of my deeds do Thou deliver me.

HOLY AND GREAT THURSDAY

Troparion. Plagal of Fourth Tone

WHEN the glorious disciples were enlightened at the washing of the feet, then Judas the ungodly one was stricken and darkened with the love of silver. And unto the lawless judges did he deliver Thee, the righteous Judge. O thou lover of money, behold thou him that for the sake thereof did hang himself; flee from that insatiable soul that dared such things against the Master. O Thou Who art good unto all, Lord, glory be to Thee.

Kontakion. Second Tone

TAKING the Bread into his hands, the betrayer stretcheth them forth secretly and receiveth the price of Him that, with His own hands, fashioned man. And Judas, the servant and deceiver, remained incorrigible.

HOLY AND GREAT FRIDAY
Troparion. Plagal of Fourth Tone

WHEN the glorious disciples were enlightened at the washing of the feet . . . *and the
rest, as on the preceding page.*

Kontakion. Plagal of Fourth Tone

COME, let us all praise Him Who was crucified for us; for Mary beheld Him on the
Tree, and said: Though Thou endurest the Cross,
yet Thou art my Son and my God.

Dismissal Hymn at the End of Matins. Fourth Tone

THOU didst ransom us from the curse of the
Law by Thy precious Blood. Nailed to the
Cross and pierced with the lance, Thou didst
pour forth immortality for men. O our Saviour, glory be to Thee.

HOLY AND GREAT SATURDAY
Dismissal Hymns. Second Tone

THE noble Joseph, taking Thine immaculate
Body down from the Tree, and having
wrapped It in pure linen and spices, laid It for
burial in a new tomb.

Glory.

WHEN Thou didst descend unto death, O
Life Immortal, then didst Thou slay
Hades with the lightning of Thy Divinity. And

when Thou didst also raise the dead out of the nethermost depths, all the powers in the Heavens cried out: O Life-giver, Christ our God, glory be to Thee.

Both now.

UNTO the myrrh-bearing women did the Angel cry out as he stood by the grave: Myrrh-oils are meet for the dead, but Christ hath proved to be a stranger to corruption.

Kontakion. Plagal of Second Tone

HE that shut up the abyss is seen to be dead, and like a mortal man, the Immortal One is wrapped in linen and myrrh, and placed in a grave. And women came to anoint Him weeping bitterly and crying out: This is the most blessed Sabbath whereon Christ, having slept, shall arise on the third day.

THE RESURRECTION

THE SERVICE OF MATINS FOR
THE HOLY AND GREAT
SUNDAY OF
PASCHA

Before the beginning of Paschal Matins, a short time before midnight, after the usual introductory prayers the choir chanteth the Canon of Holy Saturday from the Triodion, **He that once had hidden beneath the sea's waves.** *The lamps are not lit. Upon the completion of the Canon, with all lights extinguished in the temple, all the semantra are sounded. After the chanting of the Resurrection Dismissal Hymn of Second Tone,* **When Thou didst descend unto death, O Life Immortal,** *the Beautiful Gates are opened, and the priest cometh forth, holding a candle lit from the unsleeping lamp over the Holy Table. Bestowing the sacred light from his candle unto the faithful, he chanteth, in Plagal of First Tone:*

COME, receive ye light from the Unwaning ✠ Light, and glorify Christ, Who is arisen from the dead.

This is chanted in turn by the choirs until all in the church have received the light.

Then the priest taketh the sacred Gospel, and we go forth from the temple, chanting the following hymn, in Plagal of Second Tone:

A NGELS in the heavens, O Christ our Saviour, praise Thy Resurrection with hymns; deem us also who are on earth worthy to glorify Thee with a pure heart.

After we have reached the appointed place, the deacon saith: And that we may be deemed worthy to hear the holy Gospel, let us beseech the Lord our God.

The choir: Lord, have mercy. (3)

The deacon: Wisdom. Upright. Let us hear the holy Gospel.

The priest: Peace be unto all.

The choir: And to thy spirit.

The priest: The reading is from the holy Gospel according to Saint Mark.

The choir: Glory to Thee, O Lord, glory to Thee.

The deacon: Let us attend.

And the priest readeth the Second Matinal Gospel, Mark 16:1–8.

The choir: Glory to Thee, O Lord, glory to Thee.

And placing the sacred Gospel upon the stand, the priest censeth it thrice and exclaimeth:

GLORY to the Holy, and Consubstantial, and Life-creating, and Indivisible Trinity, always, now and ever, and unto the ages of ages.

The choir: **Amen.**

Then the following Troparion is chanted thrice, in Plagal of First Tone:

CHRIST is risen from the dead, by death hath He trampled down death, and on those in the graves hath He bestowed life. ✗

This hymn is repeated by the choirs after each of the following verses, which are said by the priest as he censeth the Gospel which is upon the stand:

First verse: Let God arise and let His enemies be scattered, and let them that hate Him flee from before His face.

Second verse: As smoke vanisheth, so let them vanish; as wax melteth before the fire.

Third verse: So let sinners perish at the presence of God, and let the righteous be glad.

Fourth verse: This is the day which the Lord hath made; let us rejoice and be glad therein.

Glory.

CHRIST is risen from the dead, by death hath He trampled down death, and on those in the graves hath He bestowed life.

Both now.

The hymn Christ is risen *is repeated again, and the hymn is then repeated yet again as the priest censeth the clergy and the people.*

Then the deacon saith the Great Litany: In peace let us pray to the Lord. . . .

The priest: For unto Thee is due all glory, honour, and worship, to the Father, and to the Son, and to the Holy Spirit, now and ever, and unto the ages of ages.

The choir: Amen.

Then we return to the temple, and the choir chanteth the Canon in First Tone, a composition of Saint John of Damascus, with the refrain, chanted before each of the Troparia:

Glory to Thy holy Resurrection, O Lord.

ODE ONE

Heirmos

IT is the day of Resurrection, let us be radiant, O ye peoples; Pascha, the Lord's Pascha; for Christ God hath brought us from death unto life, and from earth unto Heaven as we sing the triumphal hymn.

Troparia

LET us purify our senses and we shall behold Christ, radiant with the unapproachable light of the Resurrection, and we shall clearly hear Him say: Rejoice! as we sing the triumphal hymn.

FOR meet it is that the Heavens should rejoice, and that the earth should be glad, and that the whole world, both visible and invisible, should keep the feast; for Christ, our everlasting Joy, hath arisen.

Katavasia: It is the day of Resurrection . . .

CHRIST is risen from the dead, by death hath He trampled down death, and on those in the graves hath He bestowed life. (3)

JESUS, having risen from the grave as He foretold, hath granted us life everlasting and great mercy.

These last two hymns are chanted thus after each Ode.

Then the Small Litany, with the exclamation: For Thine is the dominion, and Thine is the kingdom, and the power, and the glory, of the Father, and of the Son, and of the Holy Spirit, now and ever, and unto the ages of ages.

The choir: Amen.

ODE THREE

Heirmos

COME, let us drink a new drink, not one marvellously brought forth from a barren rock, but the Source of incorruption, which springeth forth from the grave of Christ, in Whom we are established.

Troparia

Now are all things filled with light; Heaven and earth, and the nethermost regions of the earth. Let all creation, therefore, celebrate the arising of Christ, whereby it is established.

YESTERDAY I was buried with Thee, O Christ, and today I arise with Thine arising. Yesterday was I crucified with Thee; do Thou Thyself glorify me with Thee, O Saviour, in Thy Kingdom.

Katavasia: Come, let us drink a new drink . . .

Then the Small Litany, with the exclamation: For Thou art our God, and unto Thee do we send up glory, to the Father, and to the Son, and to the Holy Spirit, now and ever, and unto the ages of ages.

The choir: Amen.

THE HYPAKOË
Fourth Tone

WHEN they who were with Mary came, anticipating the dawn, and found the stone rolled away from the sepulchre, they heard from the Angel: Why seek ye among the dead, as though He were mortal man, Him Who abideth in everlasting light? Behold the grave-clothes. Go quickly and proclaim to the world that the Lord is risen, and hath put death to death. For He is the Son of God, Who saveth the race of man.

ODE FOUR
Heirmos

LET the Prophet Abbacum, the proclaimer of divine things, keep the divine watch with us, and show forth the radiant Angel who with resounding voice hath declared: Today doth bring salvation to the world, for Christ is risen as omnipotent.

Troparia

CHRIST revealed Himself as of the male sex when He opened the Virgin's womb, and as a mortal was He called the Lamb. Thus, without blemish is our Pascha, for He tasted not corruption; and since He is truly God, perfect was He proclaimed.

CHRIST, our blessed Crown, like unto a yearling lamb, of His own good will did sacrifice Himself for all, a Pascha of purification: and from the grave the beautiful Sun of Righteousness shone forth again upon us.

DAVID, the ancestor of our God, danced with leaping before the symbolical Ark of the Covenant. Let us also, the holy people of God, beholding the fulfilment of the symbols, rejoice in godly wise: For Christ is risen, as omnipotent.

Katavasia: Let the Prophet Abbacum . . .

Then the Small Litany, with the exclamation: For a good and man-befriending God art Thou, and unto Thee do we send up glory, to the Father, and to the Son, and to the Holy Spirit, now and ever, and unto the ages of ages.

The choir: Amen.

ODE FIVE
Heirmos

L ET us arise in the deep dawn and, instead of myrrh, offer praise to the Master; and we shall see Christ, the Sun of Righteousness, Who causeth life to dawn for all.

Troparia

W HEN those held captive in the bonds of Hades beheld Thy boundless compassion, O Christ, they hastened to the light with a joyful step, exalting the eternal Pascha.

B EARING lights, let us go forth to meet Christ, Who cometh forth from the grave like a bridegroom. And with the ranks of them that love and keep this festival, let us celebrate the saving Pascha of God.

Katavasia: Let us arise in the deep dawn . . .

Then the Small Litany, with the exclamation: **For** hallowed and glorified is Thine all-honourable and majestical Name, of the Father, and of the Son, and of the Holy Spirit, now and ever, and unto the ages of ages.

The choir: **Amen.**

ODE SIX
Heirmos

THOU didst descend into the deepest parts of the earth, and didst shatter the everlasting bars that held fast those that were fettered, O Christ. And on the third day, like Jonas from the sea monster, Thou didst arise from the grave.

Troparia

HAVING kept the seals intact, O Christ, Thou didst rise from the tomb, O Thou Who didst not break the seal of the Virgin by Thy birth; and Thou hast opened unto us the gates of Paradise.

O MY Saviour, the life-giving and unslain Sacrifice, when, as God, Thou of Thine own will, hadst offered up Thyself unto the Father, Thou didst raise up with Thyself the whole race of Adam when Thou didst rise from the grave.

Katavasia: **Thou didst descend . . .**

Then the Small Litany, with the exclamation: **For** Thou art the King of Peace, and the Saviour of our souls, and unto Thee do we send up glory, to the Father, and to the Son, and to the Holy Spirit, now and ever, and unto the ages of ages.

The choir: **Amen.**

KONTAKION
Plagal of Fourth Tone

THOUGH Thou didst descend into the grave, O Immortal One, yet didst Thou destroy the power of Hades, and didst arise as victor, O Christ God, calling to the myrrh-bearing women, Rejoice, and giving peace unto Thine Apostles, O Thou Who dost grant resurrection to the fallen.

OIKOS

THE myrrh-bearing maidens anticipated the dawn, seeking, as it were day, the Sun Who was before the sun and Who had set in the tomb, and they cried out one to another: O friends, come, let us anoint with sweet-smelling spices the life-bringing and buried Body, even that Flesh which raiseth fallen Adam, who lieth in the grave. Let us go hence, let us make haste like the Wise Men, and let us adore and offer before Him myrrh as it were a gift to Him, Who is no longer wrapped in swaddling bands, but in a winding-sheet. And let us make lamentation and cry aloud in exclamation: Arise, O Master, Thou Who dost grant resurrection to the fallen.

The Synaxarion of the Menaion, then the following:

On this, the holy and great Sunday of Pascha, we celebrate the life-bringing Resurrection of our Lord and God and Saviour Jesus Christ.

Verses

Christ, going down alone to the struggle with Hades,
Came forth again and brought with Him plenteous spoils of victory.

To Him be glory and dominion unto the ages of ages. Amen.

And straightway we chant in Plagal of Second Tone:

LET us who have beheld the Resurrection of Christ worship our holy Lord Jesus, Who is alone without sin. We worship Thy Cross, O Christ, and we praise and glorify Thy holy Resurrection. For Thou art our God, and we know none other beside Thee, and we call upon Thy Name. Come, all ye faithful, let us worship Christ's holy Resurrection, for behold, through the Cross joy hath come to the whole world. For ever blessing the Lord, we praise His Resurrection. He endured the Cross for us, and by death destroyed death. (3)

JESUS, having risen from the grave as He foretold, hath granted us life everlasting and great mercy. (3)

ODE SEVEN
Heirmos

THE only blest and most glorious God of our Fathers, Who hath redeemed the Children from the furnace, is become man, and as a mortal doth suffer, and through suffering doth clothe mortality with the grace of incorruption.

Troparia

THE godly-wise women followed after Thee in haste with sweet-smelling myrrh. But Him Whom they sought with tears as dead, they joyfully adored as the living God, and announced unto Thy disciples, O Christ, the glad tidings of the mystical Pascha.

WE celebrate the death of death, the destruction of Hades, the beginning of an everlasting life. And with leaps of joy we praise the Cause thereof, the only blest and most glorious God of our Fathers.

TRULY sacred and supremely festive is this saving night, radiant with light, the forerunner of the bright-beaming Day of the Resurrection, whereon the Timeless Light in bodily form shone from the grave for all.

Katavasia: The only blest . . .

Then the Small Litany, with the exclamation:
Blessed and glorified be the dominion of Thy Kingdom, of the Father, and of the Son, and of the Holy Spirit, now and ever, and unto the ages of ages.

The choir: Amen.

ODE EIGHT
Heirmos

THIS chosen and holy day is the first of the sabbaths, the queen and lady, the feast of feasts, and the festival of festivals, wherein we bless Christ unto the ages.

Troparia

COME, on this auspicious day of the Resurrection, let us partake of the new fruit of the vine of divine gladness and of the Kingdom of Christ, praising Him as God unto the ages.

CAST thine eyes about thee, O Sion, and behold! For lo, like divinely-radiant luminaries, thy children have assembled unto thee from the West, the North, the Sea, and the East, in thee blessing Christ unto the ages.

O FATHER Almighty, the Word, and the Spirit, one Nature in three Hypostases united, transcending essence and supremely Divine! In Thee have we been baptized, and Thee will we bless unto all the ages.

We praise, we bless, and we worship the Lord.

Katavasia: This chosen and holy day . . .

Then the Small Litany, with the exclamation: For blessed is Thy Name, and glorified is Thy Kingdom, of the Father, and of the Son, and of the Holy Spirit, now and ever, and unto the ages of ages.

The choir: Amen.

Then the deacon: Let us magnify the Theotokos and Mother of the Light, honouring her with hymns.

And the choirs chant the hymns of the ninth Ode:

ODE NINE
Megalynarion

Magnify, O my soul, Him Who suffered willingly, and was buried, and arose from the grave on the third day.

Heirmos

SHINE, shine, O new Jerusalem, for the glory of the Lord hath arisen upon thee; dance now and be glad, O Sion, and do thou exult, O pure Theotokos, in the arising of Him Whom thou didst bear.

Megalynarion

Magnify, O my soul, Christ the Giver of life, Who arose from the grave on the third day.

And again the Heirmos:

Shine, shine, O new Jerusalem . . .

Megalynarion

Christ is the new Pascha, the living sacrificial Victim, the Lamb of God that taketh away the sin of the world.

Troparion

O THY divine and beloved and most sweet voice; Thou hast truly promised that Thou wouldst be with us unto the end of the world, O Christ; and we faithful rejoice, having this as an anchor of hope.

Megalynarion

Today the whole creation is glad and doth rejoice, for Christ is risen, and Hades hath been despoiled.

And again the Troparion:

O Thy divine and beloved . . .

Glory.
Megalynarion

Magnify, O my soul, the dominion of the Undivided Godhead of Three Hypostases.

Troparion

O GREAT and most sacred Pascha, Christ;
O Wisdom and Word and Power of God!
Grant that we partake of Thee fully in the
unwaning day of Thy Kingdom.

Both now.
Megalynarion

Rejoice, O Virgin, rejoice; rejoice, O blessed
one; rejoice, O most glorified one, for thy Son
hath arisen from the grave on the third day.

And again the Troparion:

O great and most sacred Pascha . . .

Megalynarion

The Angel cried unto her that is full of grace:
O pure Virgin, rejoice, and again I say, rejoice;
for thy Son hath arisen from the grave on the
third day.

Katavasia

SHINE, shine, O new Jerusalem, for the glory
of the Lord hath arisen upon thee; dance
now and be glad, O Sion, and do thou exult,
O pure Theotokos, in the arising of Him Whom
thou didst bear.

CHRIST is risen from the dead, by death hath
He trampled down death, and on those in
the graves hath He bestowed life. (3)

Jesus, having risen from the grave as He foretold, hath granted us life everlasting and great mercy.

The foregoing hymns of the ninth Ode are given according to current usage. The traditional order for the chanting of the ninth Ode is as set forth below:

Megalynarion: Magnify, O my soul, Him Who suffered willingly, and was buried, and arose from the grave on the third day. *And the Heirmos:* Shine, shine . . .

Megalynarion: Magnify, O my soul, Him Who suffered willingly, and was buried, and arose from the grave on the third day. *And the Heirmos:* Shine, shine . . .

Megalynarion: Magnify, O my soul, Christ the Giver of life, Who arose from the grave on the third day. *And the Heirmos:* Shine, shine . . .

Megalynarion: Christ is the new Pascha, the living sacrificial Victim, the Lamb of God that taketh away the sin of the world. *And the Heirmos:* Shine, shine . . .

Megalynarion: The Angel cried unto her that is full of grace: O pure Virgin, rejoice, and again I say, rejoice; for thy Son hath arisen from the grave on the third day. *And the Troparion:* O Thy divine . . .

Megalynarion: Mary Magdalene ran unto the grave, and on seeing Christ, she questioned Him as though He were the gardener. *And the Troparion:* O Thy divine . . .

Megalynarion: A radiant Angel cried unto the women: Cease from weeping, for Christ is risen and Hades hath been despoiled. *And the Troparion:* O Thy divine . . .

Megalynarion: Roaring royally as the Lion of Judah,

having slept Thou didst awake the dead from ages past. *And the Troparion:* O Thy divine . . .

Megalynarion: O ye peoples, be glad, for Christ is risen, trampling down death and raising the dead. *And the Troparion:* O great and most sacred Pascha . . .

Megalynarion: Today the whole creation is glad and doth rejoice, for Christ is risen, and Hades hath been despoiled. *And the Troparion:* O great and most sacred Pascha . . .

Megalynarion: Today the Master despoiled Hades and raised them that from ages past were in fetters and held in grievous bondage. *And the Troparion:* O great and most sacred Pascha . . .

Glory to the Father, and to the Son, and to the Holy Spirit. *Megalynarion:* Magnify, O my soul, the dominion of the Undivided Godhead of Three Hypostases. *And the Troparion:* O great and most sacred Pascha . . .

Both now and ever, and unto the ages of ages. Amen. *Megalynarion:* Rejoice, O Virgin, rejoice; rejoice, O blessed one; rejoice, O most glorified one, for thy Son hath arisen from the grave on the third day. *And the Heirmos:* Shine, shine . . .

And again: Shine, shine ... *is chanted as the Katavasia. Then:* Christ is risen ... *thrice, and* Jesus having risen ...

Then the Small Litany, with the exclamation: For all the hosts of the Heavens praise Thee, and unto Thee do they send up glory, to the Father, and to the Son, and to the Holy Spirit, now and ever, and unto the ages of ages.

The choir: **Amen.**

EXAPOSTILARION
Second Tone

WHEN Thou hadst fallen asleep in the flesh as one mortal, O King and Lord, Thou didst rise again on the third day, raising up Adam from corruption, and abolishing death: O Pascha of incorruption! O Salvation of the world! (3)

For the Praises we allow for four verses and chant four Resurrection Stichera of the Octoëchos, and then the Stichera of Pascha with their verses, as here set forth:

FROM THE OCTOËCHOS
First Tone

Verse: Praise Him for His mighty acts, praise Him according to the multitude of His greatness.

WE praise Thy saving Passion, O Christ, and we glorify Thy Resurrection.

Verse: Praise Him with the sound of trumpet, praise Him with the psaltery and harp.

THOU Who didst endure the Cross, and didst abolish death, and didst arise from the dead: Make our life peaceful, O Lord, since Thou alone art omnipotent.

Verse: Praise Him with timbrel and dance, praise Him with strings and flute.

Thou Who didst despoil Hades, and didst raise up man by Thy Resurrection, O Christ: Deem us worthy to hymn and glorify Thee with purity of heart.

Verse: Praise Him with tuneful cymbals, praise Him with cymbals of jubilation. Let every breath praise the Lord.

Glorifying Thy God-befitting condescension, we praise Thee, O Christ; for Thou wast born of a Virgin, and yet Thou wast inseparable from the Father. Thou didst suffer as man, and didst endure the Cross willingly. Thou didst rise from the grave as though coming forth from a bridal chamber, that Thou mightest save the world. O Lord, glory be to Thee.

THE STICHERA OF PASCHA
WITH THEIR VERSES
Plagal of First Tone

Verse: Let God arise and let His enemies be scattered, and let them that hate Him flee from before His face.

A sacred Pascha hath been shown forth to us today; a new and holy Pascha, a mystic Pascha, an all-venerable Pascha, a Pascha that is Christ the Redeemer; a spotless Pascha, a great Pascha, a Pascha of the faithful, a Pascha that hath opened unto us the gates of Paradise, a Pascha that doth hallow all the faithful.

Verse: As smoke vanisheth, so let them vanish; as wax melteth before the fire.

COME from that scene, O women, bearers of good tidings, and say to Sion: Receive from us the tidings of joy, of the Resurrection of Christ. Exult, dance, and be glad, O Jerusalem, for thou hast seen Christ the King as a bridegroom come forth from the tomb.

Verse: So let sinners perish at the presence of God, and let the righteous be glad.

THE myrrh-bearing women at deep dawn drew nigh to the tomb of the Giver of life; they found an Angel sitting upon the stone, and he, addressing them, in this manner did say: Why seek ye the Living among the dead? Why mourn ye the Incorruptible amid corruption? Go, proclaim it unto His disciples.

Verse: This is the day which the Lord hath made; let us rejoice and be glad therein.

A PASCHA of delight, Pascha, the Lord's Pascha, an all-venerable Pascha hath dawned for us, a Pascha whereon let us embrace one another with joy. O Pascha, ransom from sorrow! Today Christ hath shone forth from the tomb as from a bridal chamber, and hath filled the women with joy, saying: Proclaim it unto the Apostles.

Glory; both now
Plagal of First Tone

IT is the day of Resurrection; let us be radiant for the festival, and let us embrace one another. Let us say, O brethren, even to those that hate us: Let us forgive all things on the Resurrection; and thus let us cry: Christ is risen from the dead, by death hath He trampled down death, and on those in the graves hath He bestowed life.

And the hymn **Christ is risen** *is again chanted thrice.*

THE CATECHETICAL HOMILY
OF OUR FATHER AMONG THE SAINTS
JOHN CHRYSOSTOM

Bless, Master.

IF any be pious and a lover of God, let him delight in this fair and radiant festival.

If any be an honest servant, let him come in and rejoice in the joy of his Lord.

If any have wearied himself with fasting, let him now enjoy the recompense.

If any have worked from the first hour, let him receive today his just reward.

If any have come after the third, let him feast with thankfulness.

If any have arrived after the sixth, in no wise let him be in doubt; in no way shall he suffer loss.

If any be later than the ninth, let him draw nigh, let him not waver.

If any arrive only at the eleventh, let him not be fearful for his slowness, for the Master is munificent and receiveth the last even as the first; He giveth rest to him of the eleventh even as to him who hath wrought from the first hour.

He is merciful to the last and provideth for the first; and to this one He giveth, and to that one He showeth kindness.

He receiveth their labours and acknowledgeth the purpose, and He honoureth the deed and praiseth the intention.

Wherefore, enter ye all into the joy of our Lord, and let the first and the second take part in the reward.

Ye rich and ye poor, join hands together.

Ye sober and ye heedless, do honour to this day.

Ye who fast and ye who fast not, be glad today.

The table is full: do ye all fare sumptuously.

The calf is ample: let no one go forth hungry.

Let all enjoy the banquet of Faith.

Let all enjoy the wealth of righteousness.

Let no one lament his poverty, for the Kingdom is made manifest to all.

Let no one bewail transgressions, for forgiveness hath dawned forth from the tomb.

Let no one be fearful of Death, for the death of the Saviour hath set us free.

He hath quenched Death by being subdued by Death.

He Who came down into Hades, despoiled Hades; and Hades was embittered when he tasted of Christ's Flesh.

Esaias, anticipating this, cried out and said: Hades was embittered when below he met Thee face to face.

He was embittered, for he was set at nought.

He was embittered, for he was mocked.

He was embittered, for he was slain.

He was embittered, for he was cast down.

He was embittered, for he was fettered.

He received a body, and encountered God.

He received earth, and met Heaven face to face.

He received what he saw, and fell because of what he saw not.

O Death, where is thy sting? O Hades, where is thy victory?

Risen is Christ, and thou art overthrown.

Risen is Christ, and the demons are fallen.

Risen is Christ, and the Angels rejoice.

Risen is Christ, and life doth reign.

Risen is Christ, and there is none dead in the tomb.

For Christ is raised from the dead, and is become the first-fruits of them that slept.

To Him be glory and dominion unto the ages of ages. Amen.

Then we chant the Dismissal Hymn of Saint John Chrysostom, in Plagal of Fourth Tone:

G RACE shining forth from thy mouth like a beacon hath illumined the universe, and disclosed to the world treasures of uncovetousness, and shown us the heights of humility; but whilst instructing us by thy words, O Father John Chrysostom, intercede with the Word, Christ our God, to save our souls.

The traditional rubrics indicate that, following the Glory of the Praises, It is the day of Resurrection, *the faithful exchange the paschal kiss of peace, after which is read the Catechetical Homily of Saint John Chrysostom. This is followed by the usual litanies and the dismissal which conclude the Paschal Matins, after which we begin the Paschal Liturgy.*

In current practice the Catechetical Homily of Saint John Chrysostom is read during the Divine Liturgy, and the paschal kiss of peace is exchanged during the Agape Vespers that Sunday evening.

THE PASCHAL HOURS

From the Holy and Great Sunday of Pascha until the Saturday of Renewal Week, in place of the usual Morning and Evening Prayers, the Midnight Service, the Hours, Compline, and the Prayers of Thanksgiving after Holy Communion, the following is read:

After the exclamation by the priest, we say:

CHRIST is risen from the dead, by death hath He trampled down death, and on those in the graves hath He bestowed life. (3)

Then:

LET us who have beheld the Resurrection of Christ worship our holy Lord Jesus, Who is alone without sin. We worship Thy Cross, O Christ, and we praise and glorify Thy holy Resurrection. For Thou art our God, and we know none other beside Thee, and we call upon Thy Name. Come, all ye faithful, let us worship Christ's holy Resurrection, for behold, through the Cross joy hath come to the whole world. For ever blessing the Lord, we praise His Resurrection. He endured the Cross for us, and by death destroyed death. (3)

WHEN they who were with Mary came, anticipating the dawn, and found the stone rolled away from the sepulchre, they heard from the Angel: Why seek ye among the dead, as though He were mortal man, Him Who abideth in everlasting light? Behold the grave-clothes. Go quickly and proclaim to the world that the Lord is risen, and hath put death to death. For He is the Son of God, Who saveth the race of man.

THOUGH Thou didst descend into the grave, O Immortal One, yet didst Thou destroy the power of Hades, and didst arise as victor, O Christ God, calling to the myrrh-bearing women, Rejoice, and giving peace unto Thine Apostles, O Thou Who dost grant resurrection to the fallen.

IN the grave bodily; in Hades with Thy soul, though Thou wast God; in Paradise with the thief; and on the throne with the Father and the Spirit wast Thou Who fillest all things, O Christ the Uncircumscribable.

Glory.

HOW life-giving, how much more beautiful than paradise, and truly more resplendent than any royal palace proved Thy grave, the source of our resurrection, O Christ.

Both now.

REJOICE, O sanctified and divine tabernacle of the Most High; for through thee, O Theotokos, joy is given to them that cry: Blessed art thou among women, O all-immaculate Lady.

Lord, have mercy (40). Glory; both now.

MORE honourable than the Cherubim, and beyond compare more glorious than the Seraphim, thee who without corruption gavest birth to God the Word, the very Theotokos, thee do we magnify.

In the Name of the Lord, Father, bless.

The priest: Through the prayers of our holy Fathers, Lord Jesus Christ our God, have mercy on us.

The reader: Amen.

At Compline we say the following prayer; otherwise, we proceed with Christ is risen . . . *as set forth below.*

A COMPLINE PRAYER
OF SAINT BASIL THE GREAT

BLESSED art Thou, O Almighty Master, Who hast enlightened the day with the light of the sun and hast illumined the night by the rays of fire, Who hast deemed us worthy to pass through the length of the day and draw nigh to the beginning of the night. Hearken unto our supplication, and that of all Thy people. Forgive all of us our sins, voluntary and involuntary, accept our evening entreaties, and send down the multitude of Thy mercy and compassions upon Thine inheritance. Encompass us with Thy holy Angels; arm us with the armour of Thy righteousness; surround us with Thy truth; protect us by Thy might; deliver us from every grievous circumstance and from every conspiracy of the adversary. And grant unto us that this evening together with the coming night and all the days of our life may be perfect, holy, peaceful, sinless, without stumbling and vain imaginings; by the intercessions of the holy Theotokos and of all the Saints who, from ages past, have been well-pleasing unto Thee. Amen.

And likewise again: Christ is risen . . . (3). Glory; both now. Lord, have mercy (3). Bless.

And the dismissal.

Know that from the Holy and Great Sunday of Pascha until the Feast of Pentecost, the introductory prayers, Glory to Thee, our God, glory to Thee. Heavenly King, O Comforter . . . *are not said.*

And from the Holy and Great Sunday of Pascha until the giving up of Pascha on the eve of the Feast of the Ascension, in place of Holy God, Holy Mighty, Holy Immortal . . . *and* O come, let us worship . . . *we say,* Christ is risen from the dead . . . (3).

DISMISSAL HYMNS AND
KONTAKIA OF
THE PENTECOSTARION

THOMAS SUNDAY
Dismissal Hymn. Grave Tone

WHILST the tomb was sealed, Thou, O Life, didst shine forth from the grave, O Christ God; and whilst the doors were shut, Thou didst come unto Thy disciples, O Resurrection of all, renewing through them an upright Spirit in us according to Thy great mercy.

Kontakion. Plagal of Fourth Tone

WITH his searching right hand, Thomas did probe Thy life-bestowing side, O Christ God; for when Thou didst enter whilst the doors were shut, he cried out unto Thee with the rest of the Apostles: Thou art my Lord and my God.

SUNDAY OF THE MYRRH-BEARING WOMEN
Dismissal Hymns. Second Tone

WHEN Thou didst descend unto death, O Life Immortal, then didst Thou slay Hades with the lightning of Thy Divinity. And when Thou didst also raise the dead out of the nethermost depths, all the powers in the Heavens cried out: O Life-giver, Christ our God, glory be to Thee.

THE noble Joseph, taking Thine immaculate Body down from the Tree, and having wrapped It in pure linen and spices, laid It for burial in a new tomb. But on the third day Thou didst arise, O Lord, granting great mercy to the world.

UNTO the myrrh-bearing women did the Angel cry out as he stood by the grave: Myrrh-oils are meet for the dead, but Christ hath proved to be a stranger to corruption. But cry out: The Lord is risen, granting great mercy to the world.

Kontakion. Second Tone

WHEN Thou didst cry, Rejoice, unto the Myrrh-bearers, Thou didst make the lamentation of Eve the first mother to cease by Thy Resurrection, O Christ God. And Thou didst bid Thine Apostles to preach: The Saviour is risen from the grave.

SUNDAY OF THE PARALYTIC
Kontakion. Third Tone
On this day the Virgin

As of old Thou didst raise up the paralytic, O Lord God, by Thy Godlike care and might, raise up my soul which is palsied by diverse sins and transgressions and by unseemly deeds and acts, that, being saved, I may also cry out: O Compassionate Redeemer, O Christ God, glory to Thy dominion and might.

WEDNESDAY OF MID-PENTECOST
Dismissal Hymn. Plagal of Fourth Tone

At Mid-feast give Thou my thirsty soul to drink of the waters of piety; for Thou, O Saviour, didst cry out to all: Whosoever is thirsty, let him come to Me and drink. Wherefore, O Well-spring of life, Christ our God, glory be to Thee.

Kontakion. Fourth Tone
Thou Who wast raised up

O SOVEREIGN Master and Creator of all things, O Christ our God, Thou didst cry unto those present at the Judaic Mid-feast and address them thus: Come and draw the water of immortality freely. Wherefore, we fall down before Thee and faithfully cry out: Grant Thy compassions unto us, O Lord, for Thou art truly the Well-spring of life for all.

SUNDAY OF THE SAMARITAN WOMAN
Kontakion. Plagal of Fourth Tone

HAVING come to the well in faith, the Samaritan woman beheld Thee, the Water of Wisdom, whereof having drunk abundantly, she, the renowned one, inherited the Kingdom on high for ever.

SUNDAY OF THE BLIND MAN
Kontakion. Fourth Tone
On this day Thou hast appeared

BEING blinded in the eyes of my soul, O Saviour, I come unto Thee, O Christ, as did the man who was born blind. And in repentance I cry to Thee: Of those in darkness art Thou the most radiant Light.

HOLY ASCENSION
Dismissal Hymn. Fourth Tone

THOU hast ascended in glory, O Christ our God, and gladdened Thy disciples with the promise of the Holy Spirit; and they were assured by the blessing that Thou art the Son of God and Redeemer of the world.

Kontakion. Plagal of Second Tone

WHEN Thou hadst fulfilled Thy dispensation for our sakes, uniting things on earth with the Heavens, Thou didst ascend in glory, O Christ our God, departing not hence, but remaining inseparable from us and crying unto them that love Thee: I am with you, and no one can be against you.

SUNDAY OF THE HOLY FATHERS
Dismissal Hymn. Plagal of Fourth Tone

MOST glorified art Thou, O Christ our God, Who hast established our Fathers as luminous stars upon the earth, and through them didst guide us all to the true Faith. O Most Merciful One, glory be to Thee.

Kontakion. Plagal of Fourth Tone

THE preaching of the Apostles and the doctrines of the Fathers confirmed the one Faith in the Church. And wearing the garment of truth woven from the theology on high, she rightly divideth and glorifieth the great mystery of piety.

SATURDAY OF SOULS
Dismissal Hymn. Plagal of Fourth Tone

O THOU Who by the depth of Thy wisdom dost provide all things out of love for man, and grantest unto all that which is profitable, O only Creator: Grant rest, O Lord, to the souls of Thy servants; for in Thee have they placed their hope, O our Creator and Fashioner and God.

Kontakion. Plagal of Fourth Tone

T HOSE that have departed from us and from these fleeting things, do Thou settle in the tabernacles of Thy chosen; and grant them rest with the righteous, O Immortal Saviour. For though as men they have sinned on earth, yet by the mediation of the Theotokos who gave Thee birth, do Thou, since Thou art the Lord Who art free of sin, forgive them their failings, both voluntary and involuntary, that with one voice we may cry out for them: Alleluia.

Kontakion of the Pannychis. Plagal of Fourth Tone

W ITH the Saints grant rest, O Christ, to the souls of Thy servants, where there is neither pain, nor sorrow, nor sighing, but life unending.

HOLY PENTECOST
Dismissal Hymn. Plagal of Fourth Tone

B LESSED art Thou, O Christ our God, Who hast shown forth the fishermen as supremely wise by sending down upon them the Holy Spirit, and through them didst draw the world into Thy net. O Befriender of man, glory be to Thee.

Kontakion. Plagal of Fourth Tone

O NCE, when He descended and confounded the tongues, the Most High divided the nations; and when He divided the tongues of fire, He called all men into unity; and with one accord we glorify the All-holy Spirit.

SUNDAY OF ALL SAINTS
Dismissal Hymn. Fourth Tone

A DORNED in the blood of Thy Martyrs throughout all the world as in purple and fine linen, Thy Church, through them, doth cry unto Thee, O Christ God: Send down Thy compassions upon Thy people; grant peace to Thy commonwealth, and great mercy to our souls.

Kontakion. Plagal of Fourth Tone
The Original Melody

A s first-fruits of our nature to the Planter of created things, the world presenteth the God-bearing martyred Saints in offering unto Thee, O Lord. Through their earnest entreaties, keep Thy Church in deep peace and divine tranquillity, through the pure Theotokos, O Thou Who art greatly merciful.

THE AKATHIST HYMN TO OUR SWEETEST LORD JESUS CHRIST

KONTAKION
Plagal of Fourth Tone

To Thee, the Champion Leader and Lord, the Vanquisher of Hades, I, Thy creature and servant, offer a song of praise, for Thou hast delivered me from eternal death. But as Thou hast ineffable loving-kindness, from all dangers that can be do Thou deliver me, that I may cry to Thee:

Jesus, Son of God, have mercy on me.

Ᾱ

CREATOR of Angels and Lord of Hosts, as of old Thou didst open the ear and tongue of him that was deaf and dumb, so now open my perplexed mind and tongue to praise Thy most holy Name, that I may cry to Thee:

Jesus, most wonderful, Astonishment of Angels.

Jesus, most powerful, Deliverance of Forefathers.

Jesus, most sweet, Exultation of Patriarchs.

Jesus, most glorious, Dominion of kings.

Jesus, most desired, Fulfilment of Prophets.

Jesus, most praised, Steadfastness of Martyrs.

Jesus, most gladsome, Comfort of monastics.

Jesus, most compassionate, Sweetness of presbyters.

Jesus, most merciful, Abstinence of fasters.

Jesus, most tender, Joy of the righteous.

Jesus, most pure, Sobriety of virgins.

Jesus, pre-eternal, Salvation of sinners.

Jesus, Son of God, have mercy on me.

Ɓ

SEEING the widow weeping bitterly, O Lord, Thou wast moved with compassion, and didst raise up her son as he was being carried to burial; likewise do Thou have compassion on me, O Friend of man, and raise up my soul which hath been slain by sins, as I cry aloud:

Alleluia.

Γ

SEEKING to know knowledge unknown, Philip asked: Lord, show us the Father; and Thou didst answer him: Have I been so long with you, and yet hast thou not known that I am in the Father, and the Father in Me? Wherefore, O Unsearchable One, with fear I cry to Thee:

Jesus, God before the ages.
Jesus, King almighty.
Jesus, Master long-suffering.
Jesus, Saviour most merciful.
Jesus, my Guardian most kind.
Jesus, be gracious unto my sins.
Jesus, take away mine iniquities.
Jesus, pardon mine unrighteousness.
Jesus, my Hope, forsake me not.
Jesus, my Helper, reject me not.
Jesus, my Creator, forget me not.
Jesus, my Shepherd, lose me not.
    Jesus, Son of God, have mercy on me.

Ꙙ

THOU didst endue with power from on high Thine Apostles who tarried in Jerusalem, O Jesus. Clothe Thou also me, who am stripped bare of every good work, with the warmth of Thy Holy Spirit, and grant that with love I may chant to Thee:
    Alleluia.

Є

IN the abundance of Thy mercy, O compassionate Jesus, Thou hast called publicans and sinners and unbelievers. Now despise not me who am like unto them, but accept this hymn as precious myrrh:

Jesus, invincible Power.

Jesus, unending Mercy.

Jesus, radiant Beauty.

Jesus, unspeakable Love.

Jesus, Son of the living God.

Jesus, have mercy on me, a sinner.

Jesus, hearken unto me who was conceived in iniquity.

Jesus, cleanse me who was born in sin.

Jesus, teach me who am become foolish.

Jesus, enlighten me who am darkened.

Jesus, purify me who am defiled.

Jesus, restore me, the prodigal.

    Jesus, Son of God, have mercy on me.

Z

HAVING a tempest of doubting thoughts within, Peter was sinking. But beholding Thee, O Jesus, bearing flesh and walking on the waters, he knew Thee to be the true God; and receiving the hand of salvation, he cried:

    Alleluia.

H

WHEN the blind man heard Thee, O Lord, passing by on the way, he cried: Jesus, Son of David, have mercy on me! And Thou didst call him and open his eyes. Wherefore, by Thy mercy enlighten the spiritual eyes of my heart as I cry to Thee and say:

Jesus, Creator of those on high.
Jesus, Redeemer of those below.
Jesus, Vanquisher of the nethermost powers.
Jesus, Adorner of every creature.
Jesus, Comforter of my soul.
Jesus, Enlightener of my mind.
Jesus, Gladness of my heart.
Jesus, Health of my body.
Jesus, my Saviour, save me.
Jesus, my Light, enlighten me.
Jesus, from all torment deliver me.
Jesus, save me who am unworthy.
    Jesus, Son of God, have mercy on me.

☦

As of old Thou didst redeem us from the curse of the law by Thy divinely-shed blood, O Jesus, likewise rescue us from the snares whereby the serpent hath entangled us through the passions of the flesh, through lustful incitements and perilous lethargy, as we cry to Thee:

Alleluia.

ι

BEHOLDING in human form Him Who by His hand fashioned man, and understanding Him to be their Master, the children of the Hebrews hastened with boughs to do homage, crying: Hosanna! But we offer Thee a hymn of praise, saying:

Jesus, true God.
Jesus, Son of David.
Jesus, glorious King.
Jesus, innocent Lamb.
Jesus, Shepherd most marvellous.
Jesus, Protector of mine infancy.
Jesus, Guide of my youth.
Jesus, Boast of mine old age.
Jesus, my Hope at death.
Jesus, my Life after death.
Jesus, my Comfort at Thy judgment.
Jesus, my Desire, let me not then be ashamed.
     Jesus, Son of God, have mercy on me.

К

FULFILLING the words and proclamations of the God-bearing Prophets, O Jesus, Thou didst appear on earth, and Thou Who art uncontainable didst dwell among men. Wherefore, being healed by Thy wounds, we learned to chant: Alleluia.

Λ

WHEN the light of Thy truth shone in the world, devilish delusion was driven away;

for the idols, O our Saviour, have fallen, unable to endure Thy power. But we who have received salvation cry to Thee:

Jesus, Truth dispelling falsehood.

Jesus, Light transcending every light.

Jesus, King surpassing all in strength.

Jesus, God constant in mercy.

Jesus, Bread of life, fill me who am hungry.

Jesus, Well-spring of knowledge, refresh me who am thirsty.

Jesus, Garment of gladness, clothe me who am naked.

Jesus, Haven of joy, shelter me who am un-worthy.

Jesus, Giver to those who ask, grant me mourning for my sins.

Jesus, Finder of those who seek, find my soul.

Jesus, Opener to those who knock, open my hardened heart.

Jesus, Redeemer of sinners, wash away my sins.

    Jesus, Son of God, have mercy on me.

M

DESIRING to unveil the mystery hidden from all ages, Thou wast led as a sheep to the slaughter, O Jesus, and as a voiceless lamb before its shearer. But as God, Thou didst rise from the dead and ascend with glory to Heav-

en, and together with Thyself, didst raise us up
who cry:

Alleluia.

N

NEW was the Creation which the Creator
revealed to us when He appeared, for
without seed He took flesh of a Virgin and rose
from the tomb without breaking the seal of
either, and bodily entered in unto the Apostles
whilst the doors were shut. Wherefore, marvelling at this we chant:

Jesus, Word uncontainable.
Jesus, Intelligence unfathomed.
Jesus, Power incomprehensible.
Jesus, Wisdom immeasurable.
Jesus, Divinity indepictable.
Jesus, Dominion unbounded.
Jesus, Kingdom invincible.
Jesus, Sovereignty unending.
Jesus, Strength sublime.
Jesus, Authority everlasting.
Jesus, my Creator, fashion me anew.
Jesus, my Saviour, save me.
Jesus, Son of God, have mercy on me.

Ž

SEEING the strange Incarnation of God, let us
estrange ourselves from this vain world and

raise our mind to things divine. To this end God descended to earth, that He might raise to Heaven us who cry to Him:

Alleluia.

O

WHOLLY present with those below, yet in no way separated from those above, was the Uncircumscribed One, when of His own will He suffered for us; by His death, our death He put to death, and by His Resurrection, He granted life to us who chant to Him such words as these:

Jesus, Sweetness of my heart.
Jesus, Strength of my body.
Jesus, Light of my soul.
Jesus, Alacrity of my mind.
Jesus, Gladness of my conscience.
Jesus, Hope unexcelled.
Jesus, Remembrance everlasting.
Jesus, Praise most exalted.
Jesus, my Glory most sublime.
Jesus, my Desire, reject me not.
Jesus, my Shepherd, seek me out.
Jesus, my Saviour, save me.

Jesus, Son of God, have mercy on me.

Π

ALL the orders of Angels in Heaven unceasingly glorify Thy most holy Name, O

Jesus, crying: Holy, Holy, Holy! But we sinners on earth, with our tongues of clay, chant:
Alleluia.

P

ORATORS most eloquent do we behold mute as fish before Thee, O Jesus our Saviour, for they are at a loss to explain how Thou art both perfect man and immutable God. But as for us, marvelling at this mystery, we cry with faith:

Jesus, God of gods.
Jesus, King of kings.
Jesus, Lord of lords.
Jesus, Judge of the living and the dead.
Jesus, Hope of the despairing.
Jesus, Comfort of the mourning.
Jesus, Provision of the poor.
Jesus, condemn me not according to my deeds.
Jesus, cleanse me according to Thy mercy.
Jesus, dispel my despondency.
Jesus, enlighten the thoughts of my heart.
Jesus, make me ever mindful of death.
    Jesus, Son of God, have mercy on me.

C

WISHING to save the world, O Dayspring of the Orient, Thou didst come to the dark Occident of our nature and didst humble Thyself even unto death. Wherefore, Thy Name

is exalted above every name, and from all created beings of Heaven and earth, Thou dost hear:
Alleluia.

T

Make Thy holy Angels a rampart for us, O
Christ, Thou Father of the age to come,
and cleanse us from every stain, as Thou didst
cleanse the ten lepers; and heal us, as Thou
didst heal the avaricious soul of Zacchaeus the
publican, that we may cry to Thee with compunction and say:

Jesus, Treasure unfailing.
Jesus, Wealth inexpendable.
Jesus, Food most substantial.
Jesus, Drink inexhaustible.
Jesus, Raiment of the poor.
Jesus, Defender of widows.
Jesus, Protector of orphans.
Jesus, Champion of those in hardships.
Jesus, Companion of those who journey.
Jesus, Pilot of voyagers.
Jesus, Calm Haven of the tempest-tossed.
Jesus, raise me who am fallen.
    Jesus, Son of God, have mercy on me.

V

A most compunctionate hymn do I, the
unworthy one, offer Thee, and like the

Canaanitish woman, I cry to Thee: O Jesus, have mercy on me! For not a daughter, but a flesh have I which is violently possessed by the passions and troubled with anger. Grant Thou healing to me, who cry aloud to Thee:

Alleluia.

Φ

THEE, the brilliant Beacon-light shining to those in the darkness of ignorance, did Paul once persecute; but, illumined by Thy light and perceiving the power of Thy divinely-wise voice, the fury of his soul was assuaged. In like manner, enlighten the eyes of my darkened soul as I cry such things as these:

Jesus, my King supremely powerful.
Jesus, my God omnipotent.
Jesus, my Lord immortal.
Jesus, my Creator most glorious.
Jesus, my Guide supreme in goodness.
Jesus, my Shepherd most compassionate.
Jesus, my Master rich in mercy.
Jesus, my Saviour, Friend of man.
Jesus, enlighten my senses darkened by passions.
Jesus, heal my body wounded by sins.
Jesus, cleanse my mind from vain thoughts.
Jesus, preserve my heart from evil desires.
    Jesus, Son of God, have mercy on me.

X

GRANT me Thy grace, O Jesus, Forgiver of every debt, and receive me who repent, as Thou didst receive Peter who denied Thee; and call me who am downcast, as of old Thou didst call Paul who persecuted Thee; and hearken unto me as I cry to Thee:

Alleluia.

ψ

WHILST hymning Thine Incarnation, we all praise Thee, and with Thomas we believe that Thou art our Lord and God, Who sittest with the Father, and shalt come to judge the living and the dead. Grant that I may then stand at Thy right hand, who now cry:

Jesus, King of peace, bestow Thy peace upon me.

Jesus, sweet-scented Flower, make me fragrant.

Jesus, longed-for Warmth, warm Thou me.

Jesus, eternal Temple, shelter me.

Jesus, resplendent Garment, adorn me.

Jesus, Pearl of great price, enrich me.

Jesus, precious Stone, illumine me.

Jesus, Sun of Righteousness, shine on me.

Jesus, holy Light, make me radiant.

Jesus, deliver me from infirmity of soul and body.

Jesus, rescue me from the hands of the adversary.

Jesus, save me from the everlasting torments.

 Jesus, Son of God, have mercy on me.

ω

O MOST sweet and tender-loving Jesus, receive this our small supplication, as Thou didst receive the widow's mite; and preserve Thine inheritance from all enemies, visible and invisible, from invasion of aliens, from disease and famine, from all tribulations and mortal wounds, and deliver from future torments all who cry to Thee:

 Alleluia.

The foregoing Kontakion is said thrice, then the first Oikos is recited once again:

Ѧ

CREATOR of Angels and Lord of Hosts, as of old Thou didst open the ear and tongue of him that was deaf and dumb, so now open my perplexed mind and tongue to praise Thy most holy Name, that I may cry to Thee:

Jesus, most wonderful, Astonishment of Angels.

Jesus, most powerful, Deliverance of Forefathers.

Jesus, most sweet, Exultation of Patriarchs.

Jesus, most glorious, Dominion of kings.
Jesus, most desired, Fulfilment of Prophets.
Jesus, most praised, Steadfastness of Martyrs.
Jesus, most gladsome, Comfort of monastics.
Jesus, most compassionate, Sweetness of pres-
 byters.
Jesus, most merciful, Abstinence of fasters.
Jesus, most tender, Joy of the righteous.
Jesus, most pure, Sobriety of virgins.
Jesus, pre-eternal, Salvation of sinners.
 Jesus, Son of God, have mercy on me.

KONTAKION
Plagal of Fourth Tone

To Thee, the Champion Leader and Lord, the Vanquisher of Hades, I, Thy creature and servant, offer a song of praise, for Thou hast delivered me from eternal death. But as Thou hast ineffable loving-kindness, from all dangers that can be do Thou deliver me, that I may cry to Thee:

 Jesus, Son of God, have mercy on me.

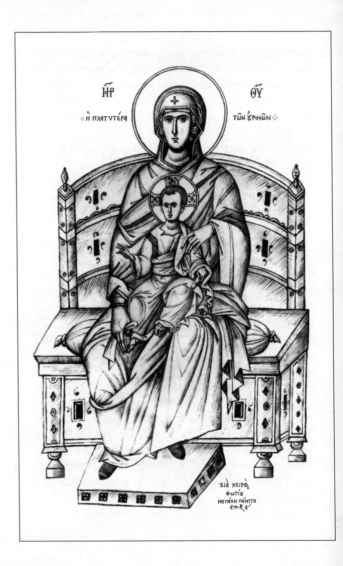

THE
AKATHIST HYMN
TO THE MOST HOLY
THEOTOKOS

A Composition of Saint Romanus
the Melodist
(✝ c. 556)

WHEN the bodiless one learned the secret command, in haste he came and stood before Joseph's dwelling, and spake unto the Maiden who knew not wedlock: The One Who hath bowed the Heavens by His descent is held and contained unchanging wholly in thee. Seeing Him receiving the form of a servant in thy womb, I stand in awe and cry to thee:
Rejoice, thou Bride unwedded.

KONTAKION
Plagal of Fourth Tone

To thee, the Champion Leader, we thy flock dedicate a feast of victory and of thanksgiving, as ones rescued out of sufferings, O Theotokos. But as thou art one with might which is invincible, from all dangers that can be do thou deliver us, that we may cry to thee:
Rejoice, thou Bride unwedded.

A

An Angel, and the chiefest among them, was sent from Heaven to cry: Rejoice! to the Mother of God. And beholding Thee, O Lord, taking bodily form, he stood in awe, and with his bodiless voice he cried aloud to her such things as these:

Rejoice, thou through whom joy shall shine forth. *Rejoice*, thou through whom the curse shall be blotted out.

Rejoice, thou the Restoration of fallen Adam. *Rejoice*, thou the Redemption of the tears of Eve.

Rejoice, Height hard to climb for human thought. *Rejoice*, Depth hard to explore, even for the eyes of Angels.

Rejoice, for thou art the Throne of the King. *Rejoice*, for thou sustainest the Sustainer of all.

Rejoice, Star that causest the Sun to appear. *Rejoice*, Womb of the divine Incarnation.

Rejoice, thou through whom creation is renewed. *Rejoice*, thou through whom the Creator becometh a babe.

Rejoice, thou Bride unwedded.

Ƃ

BEHOLDING herself in chastity, the holy one spake boldly unto Gabriel: The strangeness of thy words seemeth hard to my soul to receive; for how speakest thou of a seedless conception? crying aloud:

Alleluia.

Γ

SEEKING to know knowledge unknown, the Virgin cried to him who ministered unto her: From a chaste womb how can a Son be born? Tell thou me! Then spake he to her in fear, yet crying aloud thus:

Rejoice, thou Initiate of the ineffable counsel. *Rejoice*, thou Faith in that which demandeth silence.

Rejoice, Prelude of the miracles of Christ. *Rejoice*, Pinnacle of His doctrines.

Rejoice, heavenly Ladder whereby God came down. *Rejoice*, Bridge leading those of earth to Heaven.

Rejoice, Marvel far-famed of Angels. *Rejoice*, Wounding much-bewailed of demons.

Rejoice, thou who ineffably gavest birth to the Light. *Rejoice*, thou who didst reveal the mystery to none.

Rejoice, thou who oversoarest the knowledge of the wise. *Rejoice*, thou who enlightenest the minds of the faithful.

Rejoice, thou Bride unwedded.

A

THE power of the Most High then overshadowed her who knew not wedlock, that she might conceive, and showed forth her fruitful womb as a sweet meadow to all who desire to reap salvation, whilst chanting:

Alleluia.

E

CARRYING God in her womb, the Virgin hastened to Elizabeth, whose unborn babe straightway perceiving her salutation rejoiced; and with leaps as it were with songs, he cried out to the Theotokos:

Rejoice, Vine bearing the unfading Bloom. *Rejoice*, Land yielding the untainted Fruit.

Rejoice, thou who dost tend the man-befriending Husbandman. *Rejoice*, thou who dost blossom forth the Sower of our life.

Rejoice, Field bearing a bounty of compassions. *Rejoice*, Table laden with an abundance of mercies.

Rejoice, for thou revivest the meadow of delight. *Rejoice*, for thou preparest a haven for souls.

Rejoice, acceptable Incense of intercession. *Rejoice*, Oblation for all the world.

Rejoice, Favour of God to mortals. *Rejoice*, Access of mortals to God.

Rejoice, thou Bride unwedded.

Z

HAVING a tempest of doubting thoughts within, the chaste Joseph was troubled; for he suspected a secret union as he beheld thee unwed, O blameless one; but when he learned of thy conception through the Holy Spirit, he cried:

Alleluia.

H

ON hearing the Angels praising the incarnate presence of Christ, the shepherds hastened as to a Shepherd, and beholding Him as a spotless Lamb, pastured in Mary's womb, her they hymned, and said:

Rejoice, Mother of the Lamb and Shepherd. *Rejoice*, Fold of the rational sheep.

Rejoice, Bulwark against invisible foes. *Rejoice*, Opener of the gates of Paradise.

Rejoice, for the things of Heaven rejoice with the earth. *Rejoice*, for the things of earth join chorus with the Heavens.

Rejoice, never-silent Voice of the Apostles. *Rejoice*, never-conquered Courage of the Martyrs.

Rejoice, firm Support of the Faith. *Rejoice*, shining Token of grace.

Rejoice, thou through whom Hades was laid bare. *Rejoice*, thou through whom we are clothed with glory.

Rejoice, thou Bride unwedded.

☦

BEHOLDING the Godward-pointing Star, the Magi followed in its splendour; and holding it as a lantern, they sought thereby the mighty King. And as they approached the Unapproachable, they rejoiced and cried to Him:
Alleluia.

☦

THE sons of the Chaldees beheld in the hands of the Virgin Him Who by His hand fashioned man; and perceiving Him as Master, though He had taken the form of a servant, they hastened with gifts to do homage, and they cried out to her who is blessed:

Rejoice, Mother of the never-setting Star.
Rejoice, Dawn of the mystic Day.

Rejoice, thou who quenchest the fiery furnace of error. *Rejoice*, thou who enlightenest the initiates of the Trinity.

Rejoice, thou who didst cast down from power the inhuman tyrant. *Rejoice*, thou who didst show forth Christ, the man-befriending Lord.

Rejoice, thou who redeemest from the creeds of barbarism. *Rejoice*, thou who dost rescue from the works of mire.

Rejoice, thou who makest the worship of fire to cease. *Rejoice*, thou who makest the flame of the passions to be allayed.

Rejoice, Guide of the faithful to chastity.
Rejoice, Rejoicing of every generation.

Rejoice, thou Bride unwedded.

Κ

GOD-BEARING heralds did the Wise Men become, when they returned to Babylon; and fulfilling Thy prophecy, they preached Thee to all as the Christ, and they left Herod as a trifler, who knew not how to chant:

Alleluia.

Λ

SHINING in Egypt the illumination of truth, Thou didst dispel the darkness of falsehood;

and unable to bear Thy strength, O Saviour, her idols fell; and they that were set free therefrom cried to the Theotokos:

Rejoice, Uplifting of men. *Rejoice*, Downfall of demons.

Rejoice, thou who hast trampled upon the delusion of error. *Rejoice*, thou who hast censured the deceit of the idols.

Rejoice, Sea which drowned the noetic Pharaoh. *Rejoice*, Rock which refreshed those athirst for Life.

Rejoice, Pillar of fire, guiding those in darkness. *Rejoice*, Protection of the world, more spacious than a cloud.

Rejoice, Sustenance, successor to manna. *Rejoice*, Minister of holy joy.

Rejoice, Land of promise. *Rejoice*, thou from whence flow milk and honey.

Rejoice, thou Bride unwedded.

M

WHEN Symeon was nigh unto departing from this age of deception, Thou wast presented to him as a new-born Babe, but Thou wast recognized by him as perfect God. Wherefore, he marvelled at Thine ineffable wisdom, and cried out:

Alleluia.

N

NEW was the Creation which the Creator showed to us His creatures, when He sprang forth from the seedless womb; and He preserved it incorrupt, even as it was, that we, seeing this marvel, may praise her as we cry out:

Rejoice, Flower of incorruption. *Rejoice*, Crown of continence.

Rejoice, thou who flashest forth the type of the Resurrection. *Rejoice*, thou who showest forth the life of the Angels.

Rejoice, Tree of goodly Fruit whereby the faithful are nourished. *Rejoice*, Wood of leafy branches whereby many are sheltered.

Rejoice, thou who bearest the Guide of those astray. *Rejoice*, thou who engenderest the Redeemer of captives.

Rejoice, Supplication before the righteous Judge. *Rejoice*, Forgiveness for many transgressors.

Rejoice, Robe of confidence for the naked. *Rejoice*, Tenderness vanquishing all desire.

Rejoice, thou Bride unwedded.

Ž

SEEING a strange childbirth, let us estrange ourselves from the world by transporting our minds to Heaven; to this end the Most

High God appeared on earth a lowly man, that He might draw to the heights those who cry to Him:

Alleluia.

O

WHOLLY present with those below was the Uncircumscribed Word, yet in no way absent from those above; for this was a divine condescension and not a mere change of place; and His birth was from a Virgin chosen of God, who heard such words as these:

Rejoice, Closure of the Uncontained God. *Rejoice*, Portal of the solemn mystery.

Rejoice, doubtful Rumour of the faithless. *Rejoice*, undoubted Boast of the faithful.

Rejoice, all-holy Chariot of Him Who rideth upon the Cherubim. *Rejoice*, choicest Dwelling-place of Him Who sitteth upon the Seraphim.

Rejoice, thou who makest things that differ to agree. *Rejoice*, thou who yokest together motherhood and virginity.

Rejoice, thou through whom transgression is annulled. *Rejoice*, thou through whom Paradise is opened.

Rejoice, Key of the Kingdom of Christ. *Rejoice*, Hope of eternal blessings.

Rejoice, thou Bride unwedded.

Γ

ALL angel-kind was amazed by the great deed of Thine Incarnation; for they saw the inaccessible God as Man accessible to all, dwelling among us and hearing from all:
Alleluia.

P

ORATORS most eloquent do we behold mute as fish before thee, O Theotokos; for they are at a loss to explain how thou couldst remain a virgin and yet give birth. But as for us, marvelling at this mystery, we cry with faith:

Rejoice, Vessel of the Wisdom of God. *Rejoice*, Treasury of His providence.

Rejoice, thou who showest forth philosophers fools. *Rejoice*, thou who provest logicians illogical.

Rejoice, for the subtle disputants are confounded. *Rejoice*, for the inventors of myths are faded away.

Rejoice, thou who dost break the webs of the Athenians. *Rejoice*, thou who dost fill the nets of the Fishermen.

Rejoice, thou who dost draw us from the depths of ignorance. *Rejoice*, thou who dost enlighten many with knowledge.

Rejoice, Raft for those who desire to be

saved. *Rejoice*, Haven for those who fare on the sea of life.

    Rejoice, thou Bride unwedded.

C

WISHING to save the world, to this end did the Ruler of all come of His own will; and, though as God He is the Shepherd, for us He appeared as a Man like unto us; for by this likeness He called those of like kind, yet as God He doth hear:

    Alleluia.

T

A RAMPART art thou for virgins and all that have recourse to thee, O Theotokos and Virgin; for the Maker of heaven and earth prepared thee, O Immaculate One, and dwelt in thy womb, and taught all to cry out to thee:

Rejoice, Pillar of virginity. *Rejoice*, Gate of salvation.

Rejoice, Leader of spiritual restoration. *Rejoice*, Bestower of divine goodness.

Rejoice, for thou didst regenerate those conceived in shame. *Rejoice*, for thou didst admonish those despoiled in mind.

Rejoice, thou who dost bring to nought the corrupter of hearts. *Rejoice*, thou who dost give birth to the Sower of chastity.

Rejoice, bridal Chamber of a seedless marriage. *Rejoice,* thou who dost join the faithful to the Lord.

Rejoice, fair Nursing-mother of virgins. *Rejoice,* bridal Escort of holy souls.

Rejoice, thou Bride unwedded.

V

DEFEATED is every hymn that striveth to pay homage to the multitude of Thy many compassions; for even should we offer Thee, O holy King, odes of praise numberless as the sands, we should still have done nothing worthy of what Thou hast given unto us who cry to Thee:

Alleluia.

Φ

AS a brilliant beacon-light shining to those in darkness do we behold the holy Virgin; for she kindleth the supernal Light and leadeth all to divine knowledge; she illumineth our minds with radiance and is honoured by these our cries:

Rejoice, Ray of the spiritual Sun. *Rejoice,* Beam of the innermost Splendour.

Rejoice, Lightning, enlightening our souls. *Rejoice,* Thunder, striking down the enemy.

Rejoice, for thou dost cause the many-starred Light to dawn. *Rejoice*, for thou dost cause the ever-flowing River to gush forth.

Rejoice, thou who dost depict the image of the font. *Rejoice*, thou who dost wash away the stain of sin.

Rejoice, Laver purifying conscience. *Rejoice*, Wine-bowl pouring forth joy.

Rejoice, sweet-scented Fragrance of Christ. *Rejoice*, Life of mystic festival.

Rejoice, thou Bride unwedded.

X

WISHING to bestow His grace, He that forgiveth the ancient debts of all men came of His own will to dwell among those who had departed from His favour; and having rent asunder the handwriting against them, He heareth from all:

Alleluia.

Ψ

WHILST hymning thine Offspring, we all praise thee, O Theotokos, as a living temple; for the Lord, Who holdeth all things in His hand, dwelt in thy womb, and He hallowed and glorified thee, and taught all to cry to thee:

Rejoice, Tabernacle of God the Word. *Rejoice*, Holy one, holier than the Holies.

Rejoice, Ark made golden by the Spirit. *Rejoice*, inexhaustible Treasury of Life.

Rejoice, precious Diadem of godly kings. *Rejoice*, venerable Boast of faithful priests.

Rejoice, unshakeable Tower of the Church. *Rejoice*, impregnable Bulwark of the Kingdom.

Rejoice, thou through whom trophies are raised up. *Rejoice*, thou through whom enemies are cast down.

Rejoice, Healing of my flesh. *Rejoice*, Salvation of my soul.

Rejoice, thou Bride unwedded.

ⲱ

O ALL-HYMNED Mother, who didst bear the Word Who is more holy than all the Saints, as thou receivest this our offering, rescue us all from every calamity, and deliver from future torment those who cry with one voice:

Alleluia.

The foregoing Kontakion is said thrice, then the first Oikos is recited once again:

Ⲁ

AN Angel, and the chiefest among them, was sent from Heaven to cry: Rejoice! to the Mother of God. And beholding Thee, O Lord, taking bodily form, he stood in awe, and with his bodiless voice he cried aloud to her such things as these:

Rejoice, thou through whom joy shall shine forth. *Rejoice*, thou through whom the curse shall be blotted out.

Rejoice, thou the Restoration of fallen Adam. *Rejoice*, thou the Redemption of the tears of Eve.

Rejoice, Height hard to climb for human thought. *Rejoice*, Depth hard to explore even for the eyes of Angels.

Rejoice, for thou art the Throne of the King. *Rejoice*, for thou sustainest the Sustainer of all.

Rejoice, Star that causest the Sun to appear. *Rejoice*, Womb of the divine Incarnation.

Rejoice, thou through whom creation is renewed. *Rejoice*, thou through whom the Creator becometh a babe.

Rejoice, thou Bride unwedded.

KONTAKION
Plagal of Fourth Tone

To thee, the Champion Leader, we thy flock dedicate a feast of victory and of thanksgiving, as ones rescued out of sufferings, O Theotokos. But as thou art one with might which is invincible, from all dangers that can be do thou deliver us, that we may cry to thee:

Rejoice, thou Bride unwedded.

ΙС   ΧС

ὁ ζωο   ΔΟΤΗС

ΓΝΏΣΕ
ΣΘΕ ꞏ
ΤΗΝ ἀ
ΛΗΘΕΙ
ΑΝ Κꞏ
Η ΑΛΗ

ΘΕΙΑ ⳨
ꞋΕΛΕΥ
ΘΕΡΩ
ΣΕΙ ὗ
ΜᾶСꞏ

ΔΙΑ ΧΕΙΡΟΣ
ΦΩΤΙ8
ΑΛΞꞋ

A SUPPLICATORY CANON
TO OUR
LORD JESUS CHRIST

A Composition of the Monk
Theoctistus the Studite

Second Tone

ODE ONE

Heirmos

IN the deep abyss in times of old, all of Pharaoh's mighty host was overwhelmed by the Power supreme to arms. When the Word took on our flesh, He did utterly crush and blot out pernicious sin; for the Lord Who is most glorified hath gloriously been glorified.

O Master Christ, have mercy on Thy servants.

O MY sweetest Jesus Christ my Lord, Jesus most long-suffering, heal Thou the wounds of my soul, and make sweet my heart, Jesus, Thou most merciful, I entreat Thee, my Saviour Jesus, and beg of Thee, that being redeemed I may now magnify and glorify Thy Name.

O Master Christ, have mercy on Thy servants.

O MY sweetest Jesus Christ my Lord, Jesus, do Thou open unto me the doors of repentance, O Friend of man; and receive me as I fall down before Thee, O Saviour Jesus, and beg of Thee and most fervently implore Thee for forgiveness of mine every sin.

Glory.

O MY sweetest Jesus Christ my Lord, Jesus, do Thou snatch me from the hands of that most deceitful foe, Belial, and grant me that I may stand at the right hand of Thy dread glory, O Saviour Christ; and redeem me from the lot and portion of them on the left, O Lord.

Both now. *Theotokion*

S INCE thou gavest birth to Jesus our true God, Lady, do thou pray for us, the worthless slaves, that, by thine intercessions, Maid, O Virgin immaculate, we be rescued from grief and torment, O spotless one, and that we enjoy that glory that abideth for eternity.

ODE THREE
Heirmos

U PON the rock of faith hast Thou now confirmed me; Thou hast enlarged my mouth over mine adversaries; my spirit hath rejoiced mightily in chanting: There is none holy as our most holy God, and there is none righteous but Thee, O Lord Most High.

O Master Christ, have mercy on Thy servants.

MY Jesus, Thou Who lovest mankind, now hearken unto Thy servant crying out in compunction, and rescue me from torment and condemnation, O long-suffering Jesus, my Lord and God, O only all-merciful, sweetest Jesus Christ.

O Master Christ, have mercy on Thy servants.

RECEIVE Thy servant falling down now before Thee with tears and sighs, O Jesus, my only Jesus, and save me, O my Jesus, who am repentant, and do Thou rescue me from dread Gehenna's flames, O Master, most merciful, sweetest Jesus Christ.

Glory.

THE time that Thou didst give unto me, my Jesus, I squandered in the passions, O Lord, my Jesus. Hence, cast me not away, O my sweetest Jesus, but call me back again, Jesus, I beg of Thee, and save me, O Master, O sweetest Jesus Christ.

Both now. *Theotokion*

O VIRGIN, who didst give birth unto my Jesus, implore Him to deliver me from Gehenna; for thou alone protectest all the afflicted, O thou all-graced of God, only all-blameless Maid, and account me worthy of everlasting life.

SESSIONAL HYMN

First Tone. The soldiers standing guard

O SAVIOUR, Jesus, Thou wast the Prodigal's saviour. O Saviour, Jesus, Thou didst accept the base Harlot. Have mercy on me now also, O Jesus most merciful. Save, have pity, O my Jesus, O Benefactor, even as Thou tookest pity once on Manasses, O Jesus, Thou Friend of man.

ODE FOUR

Heirmos

N EITHER an angel, nor yet an ambassador, O my Lord, but Thyself incarnate camest from a Virgin and holy Maid, rescuing me, the whole man. Wherefore, I cry to Thee: Glory to Thy power, O Lord my God.

O Master Christ, have mercy on Thy servants.

G RANT healing unto the wounds of my soul, O Jesus my Lord, I entreat Thee, O my Jesus; and do Thou snatch me from the hands of soul-harming Belial. O my compassionate Jesus, hasten Thou to deliver me.

O Master Christ, have mercy on Thy servants.

O SWEETEST and all-compassionate Lord Jesus, I have sinned; O my Jesus, save me who flee to Thy shelter and love for man, Jesus, most long-suffering, and make me worthy, O Jesus, of Thy Kingdom for evermore.

Glory.

No one, O my Saviour Jesus, hath ever sinned as have I, even I, the hapless one; and I fall prostrate and pray to Thee: O my Jesus, rescue me, save me, bequeath me unending life, O Jesus, my Lord and God.

Both now. *Theotokion*

O ALL-HYMNED one, who didst give birth to Jesus, my Lord and God, make entreaty unto Him that He deliver from torment all them who chant in praise of thee and who acclaim thee correctly as the Mother of God, O Maid.

ODE FIVE

Heirmos

THOU art the Light of them that lie in darkness and the Salvation of all the despairing, O Christ my Saviour. O King of Peace, to Thee do I rise up early. With Thy radiance do Thou enlighten me; for, save Thee, I do not acknowledge another God.

O Master Christ, have mercy on Thy servants.

THOU art the light of my mind, O Jesus, and the salvation of my poor despairing soul, O Christ my Saviour. Wherefore, my Jesus, do Thou save me from torment and Gehenna; for, lo, I cry to Thee: Rescue me, the wretch, O my Jesus, my Christ and God.

O Master Christ, have mercy on Thy servants.

UTTERLY cast down in profligate passions, O Christ my Jesus, from the depths I cry unto Thee, my Saviour: Stretch forth to me a helping hand, O my Jesus, draw me out; for, lo, I now cry to Thee: Rescue me, the wretch, O my Jesus, my Christ and God.

Glory.

CARRYING about a defiled mind, I call unto Thee, O Jesus: Cleanse me of the defilement of my transgressions; make haste, redeem me, who have fallen down headlong into depths of sin through mine ignorance, and save me, O Saviour, my Jesus, I beg of Thee.

Both now. *Theotokion*

O VIRGIN Maid, who didst give birth to Jesus, my God and Saviour, fervently implore Him now to deliver Orthodox faithful, cenobites, and monastics, and to save from Gehenna them that cry: We know none but thee as a certain protection, Maid.

ODE SIX
Heirmos

COMPASSED by the abyss of my many sins, I invoke the boundless abyss and unfathomed deep of Thy compassion, O my Christ: Raise me out of corruption, O Lord my God.

O Master Christ, have mercy on Thy servants.

O MY Jesus, my merciful Christ and Lord, do Thou now accept me who truly confess to Thee and save me, O Lord Jesus Christ; snatch me out of corruption, I beg of Thee.

O Master Christ, have mercy on Thy servants.

O MY Jesus, none other hath ever been such a shameless prodigal as I, the wretched one, O man-befriending Jesus Christ; but do Thou, O my Jesus, now rescue me.

Glory.

O MY Jesus, in passions and evil deeds, I surpass the Harlot, the Thief, and the Publican, the Prodigal, the Ninevites, and Manasses, O Jesus, my Lord and God.

Both now. *Theotokion*

SINCE thou broughtest forth Jesus, my Christ and God, O pure Virgin who art alone free of every stain, now with the hyssop of thy prayers, do thou purify me who am all defiled.

KONTAKION
Fourth Tone. On this day Thou hast appeared

O THOU Light of all the world, my sweetest Jesus, O my Lord, illuminate the eyes of my benighted soul with the divine splendour of Thy light, that I may praise Thee, Who art the Unwaning Light.

ODE SEVEN
Heirmos

IN Deira's great plain, where the golden image was shown adoration, Thy three courageous Youths despised the impious decree issued by the king. Cast into the flames, they were sprinkled with Thy dew and they cried in chant: Blessed art Thou, O Lord our God, even the God of our Fathers.

O Master Christ, have mercy on Thy servants.

O JESUS, the Christ, none on earth from ages past hath ever wrought sins as I, the wretched and prodigal, have wrought, O Jesus, my Lord and God. Hence, I cry to Thee, O my

Jesus; have compassion on me who sing: Blessed art Thou, O Lord our God, even the God of our Fathers.

O Master Christ, have mercy on Thy servants.

O JESUS, the Christ, do Thou nail down my soul with Thy fear, I cry out, and do Thou guide me to Thy calm haven, O my Lord Jesus, I beg of Thee, that, saved and redeemed, I may hymn Thee, O compassionate Jesus Christ: Blessed art Thou, O Lord our God, even the God of our Fathers.

Glory.

O JESUS, the Christ, lo, ten thousand times have I, the vile and foul one, promised to offer Thee repentance, Lord, but I, the wretched, have lied to Thee. Hence, I cry to Thee, O my Jesus: Do Thou grant light unto my soul, which yet remaineth unfeeling, O Christ, the God of our Fathers.

Both now. *Theotokion*

SINCE thou didst give birth unto Jesus awesomely and above nature implore Him, O all-blameless Virgin Maid, that He forgive mine unnatural sins and vile transgressions, O pure one, that when saved, I might cry in praise: Blessed art thou who in the flesh hast given birth unto Christ God.

ODE EIGHT
Heirmos

To the Lord God Who did descend to the Hebrew Children in the fiery furnace and did transform the flames and the burning heat into dew, chant praises and hymns, O all ye works of His, and exalt Him greatly to ages and all ages.

O Master Christ, have mercy on Thy servants.

Jesus, I beg Thee and implore: As Thou didst redeem the harlot from her great sins, O my Jesus, so likewise do Thou redeem me, I pray, O Christ, my Lord Jesus, my King and God; and do Thou now cleanse my defiled soul, O Jesus.

O Master Christ, have mercy on Thy servants.

My Jesus, I have yielded to the irrational and brute pleasures, O Jesus, and, lo, I the wretch miserably am become like the beasts and truly am proven irrational. From this grievous state do Thou save me, O my Jesus.

Glory.

O Jesus, I did fall into the foul hands of soul-corrupting thieves, O Jesus, and am stripped of the garment woven for me by my

God; and covered with wounds, I lie prostrate now. Pour Thy healing oil and wine on me, O Jesus.

Both now. *Theotokion*

O THEOTOKOS, Bride of God, in a manner that surpasseth understanding, thou didst bear Christ my God; hence, ever entreat Him to save from perils, O Mary, all them that now serve thee and acclaim thee, the Maid who knew not wedlock.

ODE NINE
Heirmos

WITH one accord, let us faithful laud with hymns God the Word, Who came forth from God, and Who ineffably took on flesh from a pure Virgin for us and in wisdom past telling descended to make Adam new again, who by eating fell grievously down into corruption's pits.

O Master Christ, have mercy on Thy servants.

WITH wicked deeds most unseemly, full of shame, O my Jesus, I have surpassed the Publican in sins, wicked Manasses, the Prodigal Son, with the Thief and the Harlot, O Jesus, my compassionate Lord Christ. But forestall me, O Jesus, and save me, O sweetest Christ.

O Master Christ, have mercy on Thy servants.

I HAVE outdone with my passions all the children of Adam, all that have sinned before the Law, O Christ, those in the Law, and those after the Law and in Grace, O my Jesus; I miserably have sinned above them all. Yet, O Lord, in Thy judgments, deliver me, the wretch, O Christ.

Glory.

FROM Thine ineffable glory may I not be separated, nor may the portion on the left, O Christ, fall to me, O sweetest Jesus my Lord. Setting me at Thy right hand with all Thy sheep, O Jesus, Lord and God, grant me rest, O my Jesus, O Christ God most compassionate.

Both now. *Theotokion*

THOU who alone didst bear Jesus, O all-pure Theotokos, Mary, thou Virgin who didst not know man, plead thou with Him as thy Maker and Son to be gracious to all, so that we who have recourse to thee be spared from temptations and perils, and from the fire that is to come.

And the following stichera, a composition of the same Theoctistus:

Plagal of Second Tone. Having laid up all their hope

O MY sweetest Jesus, Thou the Joy and Gladness of my soul, Jesus, Thou the cleansing of my mind, O my Master and Lord most merciful: Jesus, do Thou save me, O Jesus my Saviour; O my Jesus, Thou Almighty One, do not abandon me; O my Saviour Jesus, have mercy and deliver me from punishment, O my Jesus, and deem me worthy of the lot of the choir of all Thy blessed and chosen ones, O Jesus, Thou Friend of man.

O MY sweetest Jesus, Thou the glory of the Apostles, O my Jesus, Thou the boast of the Martyrs, Master Who art omnipotent: O Jesus, do Thou save me, O Jesus my Saviour; O my Jesus, Thou most comely One, do Thou have mercy on me, O Saviour Jesus, who run to Thee, by the entreaties of her that bare Thee and, O Jesus, of all Thy Saints, and of all the Prophets, O Saviour Jesus, and do Thou vouchsafe the Paradise of delight to me, O Jesus, Thou Friend of man.

Glory.

O MY sweetest Jesus, Thou the glory of the monastics, O long-suffering Jesus, Thou the ascetics' blest adornment and great delight: O Jesus, do Thou save me, O Jesus my Saviour; O my Jesus Thou supremely good, snatch me out of the hand of the dragon, O Saviour Jesus Christ, and do Thou free me from his snares, O my Saviour Jesus, and do Thou now lead me up, my Saviour, out of the lowest pit, O Jesus, and number me, O Jesus, with Thy sheep at Thy holy, blessed right hand.

Both now. *Theotokion*

O ENTRUST me not, I pray, to any human protection, O our Lady, holy one, but do thou accept the prayer of thy supplicant. Sorrow hath fettered me, and I am unable to endure and bear the demons' darts; a shelter have I not, neither place to run, I, the wretched one; embattled from all sides am I, and no consolation have I but thee. Mistress of creation, protection and hope of faithful ones: Turn not away when I pray to thee; do that which will profit me.

A PRAYER
TO OUR LORD JESUS CHRIST

O MASTER Christ God, Who by Thy Passion hast healed my passions, and by Thy wounds hast healed my wounds: do Thou grant tears of compunction unto me who have greatly offended; do Thou temper my body with the fragrance of Thy life-creating Body, and sweeten my soul with Thy precious Blood, taking away the bitterness which the contending adversary hath made me to drink. Lift my mind up unto Thee, since it hath been drawn down below, and lead me up from the pit of destruction; for I have not repentance, I have not compunction, I have not a tear of supplication as children which shall lead me up unto mine own inheritance. I have been darkened in mind by the passions of life and I am not able to look up unto Thee in my travail; I cannot rouse myself to fervour with tears of love for Thee. But, O Master, Lord Jesus Christ, Thou Treasury of good things, grant complete repentance unto me, and a suffering heart that shall seek Thee out. Grant Thy grace unto me and renew in me the likenesses of Thine image. I have abandoned Thee; do Thou not abandon me. Come Thou forth and seek me out, lead me forth into Thy pasture, number me together with the sheep of Thine elect flock, and nourish me together with them on the verdure of Thy divine Mysteries, by the intercessions of Thine all-pure Mother and of all Thy Saints. Amen.

THE SERVICE OF
THE SMALL SUPPLICATORY CANON TO THE
MOST HOLY THEOTOKOS

A Composition of Theosterictus the Monk
(But, according to some, by Theophanes)

The Small Supplicatory Canon is chanted in every calamity and affliction of soul, as well as during the first fourteen days of August (that is, the Fast of the Mother of God), alternately with the Great Supplicatory Canon.

The priest: **Blessed is our God, always, now and ever, and unto the ages of ages.**

The reader: **Amen.** *But if there be no priest, then:* **Through the prayers of our holy Fathers, Lord Jesus Christ our God, have mercy on us. Amen.**

The priest, but if there be no priest, then the reader: **Glory to Thee, our God, glory to Thee.**

Heavenly King. *(For the complete text of the introductory prayers, see pages 17–18.)*

The reader: Holy God. All-holy Trinity. Our Father.

The priest: For Thine is the kingdom, and the power, and the glory, of the Father, and of the Son, and of the Holy Spirit, now and ever, and unto the ages of ages.

The reader: Amen. *But if there be no priest, then the reader:* Through the prayers of our holy Fathers, Lord Jesus Christ our God, have mercy on us. Amen.

Lord, have mercy (12). Glory; both now.

O come, let us worship and fall down before our King and God.

O come, let us worship and fall down before Christ, our King and God.

O come, let us worship and fall down before Him, Christ the King and our God.

PSALM 142

O LORD, hear my prayer, give ear unto my supplication in Thy truth; hearken unto me in Thy righteousness.

And enter not into judgment with Thy servant, for in Thy sight shall no man living be justified.

For the enemy hath persecuted my soul; he hath humbled my life down to the earth.

He hath sat me in darkness as those that have been long dead, and my spirit within me is become despondent; within me my heart is troubled.

I remembered days of old, I meditated on all Thy works, I pondered on the creations of Thy hands.

I stretched forth my hands unto Thee; my soul thirsteth after Thee like a waterless land.

Quickly hear me, O Lord; my spirit hath fainted away.

Turn not Thy face away from me, lest I be like unto them that go down into the pit.

Cause me to hear Thy mercy in the morning; for in Thee have I put my hope.

Cause me to know, O Lord, the way wherein I should walk; for unto Thee have I lifted up my soul.

Rescue me from mine enemies, O Lord; unto Thee have I fled for refuge. Teach me to do Thy will, for Thou art my God.

Thy good Spirit shall lead me in the land of uprightness; for Thy Name's sake, O Lord, shalt Thou quicken me.

In Thy righteousness shalt Thou bring my soul out of affliction, and in Thy mercy shalt Thou utterly destroy mine enemies.

And Thou shalt cut off all them that afflict my soul, for I am Thy servant.

And straightway God is the Lord *is chanted by the choir:*

Fourth Tone

G OD is the Lord, and hath appeared unto us; blessed is He that cometh in the Name of the Lord.

And the same is also chanted after each of the following verses:

Verse: O give thanks unto the Lord, and call upon His holy Name.

Verse: All the nations compassed me round about, and by the Name of the Lord I warded them off.

Verse: This is the Lord's doing, and it is marvellous in our eyes.

Then the following Troparia:
Fourth Tone. Thou Who wast raised up

T O God's Birthgiver let us run now most earnestly, we sinners all and wretched ones, and fall prostrate in repentance, calling from the depths of our souls: Lady, come unto our aid, have compassion upon us; hasten thou, for we are lost in a throng of transgressions; turn not thy servants away with empty hands, for thee alone do we have as our only hope.

Glory.
Repeat the Same.

Both now.

O THEOTOKOS, we shall not cease from speaking of all thy mighty acts, all we the unworthy ones; for if thou hadst not stood to intercede for us, who would have delivered us from such numerous dangers? Who would have preserved us all until now in true freedom? O Lady, we shall not turn away from thee; for thou dost always save thy servants from all manner of grief.

PSALM 50

HAVE mercy on me, O God, according to Thy great mercy; and according to the multitude of Thy compassions blot out my transgression.

Wash me thoroughly from mine iniquity, and cleanse me from my sin.

For I know mine iniquity, and my sin is ever before me.

Against Thee only have I sinned and done this evil before Thee, that Thou mightest be justified in Thy words, and prevail when Thou art judged.

For behold, I was conceived in iniquities, and in sins did my mother bear me.

For behold, Thou hast loved truth; the hidden and secret things of Thy wisdom hast Thou made manifest unto me.

Thou shalt sprinkle me with hyssop, and I shall be made clean; Thou shalt wash me, and I shall be made whiter than snow.

Thou shalt make me to hear joy and gladness; the bones that be humbled, they shall rejoice.

Turn Thy face away from my sins, and blot out all mine iniquities.

Create in me a clean heart, O God, and renew a right spirit within me.

Cast me not away from Thy presence, and take not Thy Holy Spirit from me.

Restore unto me the joy of Thy salvation, and with Thy governing Spirit establish me.

I shall teach transgressors Thy ways, and the ungodly shall turn back unto Thee.

Deliver me from blood-guiltiness, O God, Thou God of my salvation; my tongue shall rejoice in Thy righteousness.

O Lord, Thou shalt open my lips, and my mouth shall declare Thy praise.

For if Thou hadst desired sacrifice, I had given it; with whole-burnt offerings Thou shalt not be pleased.

A sacrifice unto God is a broken spirit; a heart that is broken and humbled God will not despise.

Do good, O Lord, in Thy good pleasure unto Sion, and let the walls of Jerusalem be builded.

Then shalt Thou be pleased with a sacrifice of

righteousness, with oblation and whole-burnt offerings.

Then shall they offer bullocks upon Thine altar.

Then we chant the Canon, in Plagal of Fourth Tone:

ODE ONE
Heirmos

TRAVERSING the water as on dry land, and thereby escaping from the toils of Egypt's land, the Israelites cried aloud, proclaiming: Unto our God and Redeemer let us now sing.

Most Holy Mother of God, save us.

BY many temptations am I distressed; in search of salvation, unto thee have I taken flight; O Mother of the Word, thou Ever-virgin, from all ordeals and afflictions deliver me.

Most Holy Mother of God, save us.

ATTACKS of the passions disquiet me; my soul to repletion hath been filled with despondency; bestill them, O Maiden, with the calmness of thine own Son and thy God, O all-blameless one.

Glory.

TO Christ God, the Saviour, thou gavest birth; I beg thee, O Virgin, from afflictions deliver me; for now unto thee I flee for refuge, bringing to thee both my soul and my reasoning.

Both now.

DISEASED is my body and my soul, do thou make me worthy of divine guidance and thy care, O thou who alone art God's Mother, for thou art good and the Birthgiver of the Good.

ODE THREE
Heirmos

OF the vault of the heavens art Thou, O Lord, Fashioner; so, too, of the Church art Thou founder; do Thou establish me in unfeigned love for Thee, Who art the height of things sought for, and staff of the faithful, O Thou only Friend of man.

Most Holy Mother of God, save us.

I HAVE thee as the shelter and the defence of my life, thee, the Theotokos and Virgin; pilot and govern me into thy sheltered port, for thou art author of good things and staff of the faithful, O thou only lauded one.

Most Holy Mother of God, save us.

I BESEECH thee, O Virgin, do thou dispel far from me all of the distress of despair and turbulence in my soul; for thou, O Bride of God, hast given birth to the Lord Christ Who is Prince of Peace, O thou only all-blameless one.

Glory.

SINCE thou gavest birth unto our Benefactor, the cause of good, from the wealth of thy loving-kindness do thou pour forth on all; for thou canst do all things, since thou didst bear Christ, the One Who is mighty in power; for blessed of God art thou.

Both now.

WITH most grievous diseases and with corrupt passions too, I am put to trial, O Virgin; come thou unto mine aid; for I know thee to be an inexhaustible treasure of unfailing healing, O only all-blameless one.

PRESERVE and save, O Theotokos, thy servants from every danger; after God do all of us for refuge flee unto thee; a firm rampart art thou and our protection.

IN thy good will, look thou on me, O all-hymned Theotokos; and do thou behold my body's grievous infirmity, and heal thou the cause of my soul's sorrow.

Then the priest commemorateth those for whom the Supplication is chanted:

Have mercy on us, O God, according to Thy great mercy, we pray Thee, hearken and have mercy.

The choir, after each petition:
Lord, have mercy. (3)

Again we pray for pious and Orthodox Christians.

Again we pray for our Bishop (*Name*), and for all our brotherhood (*or* sisterhood) in Christ.

Again we pray for mercy, life, peace, health, salvation, visitation, pardon and remission of the sins of the servants of God, all pious and Orthodox Christians who dwell and sojourn in this city, the parishioners and benefactors of this holy temple, and all that serve, chant, labour and gather herein; and for the servants of God (*Names*), and for the forgiveness of their every transgression, both voluntary and involuntary.

For a merciful and man-befriending God art Thou, and unto Thee do we send up glory, to the Father, and to the Son, and to the Holy Spirit, now and ever, and unto the ages of ages.

The choir: Amen.

After these petitions, we chant the following Sessional Hymn:

Second Tone

O FERVENT advocate, invincible battlement, fountain of mercy, and sheltering retreat for the world, earnestly we cry to thee: Lady Mother of God, hasten thou, and save us from all imperilment; for thou alone art our speedy protectress.

ODE FOUR

Heirmos

I HAVE hearkened and heard, O Lord, of Thy dispensation's most awesome mystery; and I came to knowledge of Thy works, and I sang the praise of Thy Divinity.

Most Holy Mother of God, save us.

L ULL the tempest of all my sins, and bestill the raging of passions with thy calm; for progenitress art thou of Him Who is Lord and Helmsman, O thou Bride of God.

Most Holy Mother of God, save us.

O BESTOW, out of the abyss of thy great compassion, on me thy supplicant; thou hast brought forth One compassionate Who is Saviour of all who sing hymns to thee.

Glory.

WHILE delighting, O spotless one, in thy many favours, a hymn of thankfulness do we all raise up in song to thee, knowing thee to be the Mother of our God.

Both now.

HAVING thee as our staff and hope, and as our salvation's unshaken battlement, from all manner of adversity are we then redeemed, O thou all-lauded one.

ODE FIVE
Heirmos

LORD, enlighten us by Thy precepts and by Thy commands; and by the power of Thy lofty arm bestow Thy peace upon us all, since Thou art Friend of man.

Most Holy Mother of God, save us.

PURE one, fill my heart with rejoicing unto plenitude; and grant thine undefiled felicity, since thou didst give birth unto Him Who is the cause of joy.

Most Holy Mother of God, save us.

COME, deliver us out of dangers, O pure Mother of God, since thou art mother of deliverance, and of the peace which doth surpass all human reasoning.

Glory.

DISSIPATE the gloom of my trespasses, O Bride of God, with the clear brightness of thy radiance; for thou didst bear the Light divine which was before all time.

Both now.

HEAL me, O pure one, of the sickness which the passions bring, and make me worthy of thy guardiancy, and by thy prayers and intercessions grant thou health to me.

ODE SIX
Heirmos

ENTREATY do I pour forth unto the Lord, and to Him do I proclaim all my sorrows, for many woes fill my heart to repletion, and lo, my life unto Hades hath now drawn nigh; like Jonas do I pray to Thee: Raise me up from corruption, O Lord my God.

Most Holy Mother of God, save us.

MY nature, held by corruption and by death, hath He saved from out of death and corruption, for unto death He Himself hath submitted. Wherefore, O Virgin, do thou intercede with Him Who is in truth thy Lord and Son to redeem me from enemies' wickedness.

Most Holy Mother of God, save us.

I KNOW thee as the protection of my life and most safe fortification, O Virgin; disperse the horde of my many temptations, and put to silence demonic audacity; unceasingly I pray to thee: From corruption of passions deliver me.

Glory.

A BULWARK of safe retreat art thou to us, and of souls art thou the perfect salvation, and a relief in distresses, O Maiden; and in thy light do we ever exult with joy. O Lady, do thou also now from all passions and perils deliver us.

Both now.

B EDRIDDEN, I lie supine with sickness now, and no healing for my flesh is existent except for thee, who didst bear the world's Saviour, our God, the Healer of every infirmity; I pray to thee, for thou art good: From corruption of illnesses raise me up.

P RESERVE and save, O Theotokos, thy servants from every danger; after God do all of us for refuge flee unto thee; a firm rampart art thou and our protection.

O SPOTLESS one, who inexpressibly in the last days didst by a word bring forth the Word; do thou make request of Him, as one who hath motherly boldness.

The priest maketh commemoration as before.

After the petitions, we chant the Kontakion, in Second Tone:

O PROTECTION of Christians that cannot be put to shame, mediation unto the Creator most constant: O despise not the suppliant voices of those who have sinned; but be thou quick, O good one, to come unto our aid, who in faith cry unto thee: Hasten to intercession, and speed thou to make supplication, thou who dost ever protect, O Theotokos, them that honour thee.

Then we chant the First Antiphon of the Hymns of Ascent of Fourth Tone:

FROM my youth do many passions war against me; but do Thou Thyself defend and save me, O my Saviour. (2)

YE haters of Sion shall be shamed by the Lord; for, like grass, by the fire shall ye be withered. (2)

Glory.

IN the Holy Spirit every soul is quickened, and through cleansing is exalted and made radiant by the Triple Unity in a hidden sacred manner.

Both now.

B Y the Holy Spirit the streams of grace gush forth, watering all creation for the begetting of life.

And straightway we chant the Prokeimenon:

I shall commemorate thy name in every generation and generation. (2)

Verse: Hearken, O daughter, and see, and incline thine ear; and forget thine own people, and thy father's house; and the King shall greatly desire thy beauty.

And we chant the Prokeimenon once again.

The priest: And that we may be deemed worthy to hear the holy Gospel, let us beseech the Lord our God.

The choir: Lord, have mercy. (3)

The priest: Wisdom. Upright. Let us hear the holy Gospel. Peace be unto all.

The choir: And to thy spirit.

The priest: The reading is from the holy Gospel according to Saint Luke.

The choir: Glory to Thee, O Lord, glory to Thee.

The priest: Let us attend.

(Luke 1:39–49, 56)

IN those days, Mary arose and went into the hill country with haste, into a city of Judah; and entered into the house of Zacharias and greeted Elizabeth. And it came to pass that, when Elizabeth heard the salutation of Mary, the babe leaped in her womb; and Elizabeth was filled with the Holy Spirit. And she spake out with a loud voice, and said: Blessed art thou among women, and blessed is the fruit of thy womb. And whence is this to me, that the mother of my Lord should come to me? For, behold, as soon as the voice of thy salutation sounded in mine ears, the babe leaped in my womb for joy. And blessed is she that believed; for there shall be a fulfilment of those things which have been spoken to her from the Lord. And Mary said: My soul doth magnify the Lord, and my spirit hath rejoiced in God my Saviour. For He hath looked upon the lowliness of His handmaiden; for behold, from hence-forth all generations shall call me blessed. For the Mighty One hath done great things to me, and holy is His Name. And Mary abode with her about three months, and returned to her own house.

The choir: Glory to Thee, O Lord, glory to Thee.

Glory. *Second Tone*

O Father, Word, and Spirit, the Trinity in Unity: blot out the multitude of mine offences.

Both now. *Theotokion*

By the intercessions of the Theotokos, O Merciful One, blot out the multitude of mine offences.

Verse: Have mercy on me, O God, according to Thy great mercy; and according to the multitude of Thy compassions blot out my transgression.

Plagal of Second Tone. Having laid up all their hope

O ENTRUST me not, I pray, to any human protection, O our Lady, holy one, but do thou accept the prayer of thy supplicant. Sorrow hath fettered me, and I am unable to endure and bear the demons' darts; a shelter have I not, neither place to run, I, the wretched one; embattled from all sides am I, and no consolation have I but thee. Mistress of creation, protection and hope of faithful ones: Turn not away when I pray to thee; do that which will profit me.

Theotokia

FROM thee is no one turned away ashamed and empty who doth run to thee for refuge,

O pure Virgin Theotokos; but he asketh the favour and receiveth the gift from thee, unto the profit of his own request.

THE transformation of the afflicted and the relief of those in sickness art thou in truth, O Virgin Theotokos; save thy people and thy flock, thou who art the peace of the embattled, and who art the calm of the storm-driven, the only protectress of those who believe.

The priest:

SAVE, O God, Thy people, and bless Thine inheritance; visit Thy world with mercy and compassions; exalt the horn of Orthodox Christians, and send down upon us Thy rich mercies: by the intercessions of our all-immaculate Lady Theotokos and Ever-virgin Mary; by the power of the honoured and life-giving Cross; by the protection of the venerable, heavenly Bodiless Powers; by the supplications of the venerable, glorious Prophet, Forerunner, and Baptist John; of the holy, glorious, and all-famed Apostles; of our Fathers among the Saints, the great Hierarchs and universal Teachers, Basil the Great, Gregory the Theologian, and John Chrysostom; Athanasius, Cyril, and John the Almsgiver, Patriarchs of Alexandria; Nicholas, Archbishop of Myra, and Spyridon, Bishop of Trimythus, the wonderworkers; of the holy, glorious Great Martyrs, George the Trophy-bearer, Demetrius the Myrrh-streamer, Theodore the Tyro, Theodore the Commander, and Menas the wonderworker; of the Sacred Martyrs Haralampus and Eleutherius; of the holy, glorious and triumphantly victorious Martyrs; of our righteous and God-bearing Fathers; of (*the Saint to whom the temple is dedicated*); of the holy, righteous Ancestors of God Joachim and Anna; of (*the Saints of the day*) whose memory we keep, and of all Thy Saints: We beseech Thee, Thou only greatly merciful God, hearken unto us sinners who pray unto Thee, and have mercy on us.

The choir: **Lord, have mercy.** (12)

The priest: **By the mercy and compassions and love for man of Thine Only-begotten Son, with Whom Thou art blessed, together with Thine All-holy and good and life-creating Spirit, now and ever, and unto the ages of ages.**

The choir: **Amen.**

And we complete the remaining Odes of the Canon:

ODE SEVEN
Heirmos

ONCE from out of Judea did the Children go down to the land of Babylon; the fire of the furnace they trampled down while chanting by their faith in the Trinity: O God of our Fathers, blessed art Thou.

Most Holy Mother of God, save us.

HAVING willed thus, O Saviour, to dispense our salvation in Thine economy, Thou dweltest in the Maid's womb, and unto all creation as protectress didst show her forth; O God of our Fathers, blessed art Thou.

Most Holy Mother of God, save us.

MAKE request, O pure Mother, to thy Son Who hath willed to grant mercy unto us, to rescue from transgressions and from the soul's defilement those who cry out most faithfully: O God of our Fathers, blessed art Thou.

Glory.

A FOUNT of incorruption and a tower of safety is she who gave Thee birth; a treasure of salvation and portal of repentance hast Thou proved her to them that shout: O God of our Fathers, blessed art Thou.

Both now.

DEIGN to grant restoration from diseases of body and soul to those who run to thy divine protection with faith, O Theotokos, and thus grant them recovery; for Mother of Christ our Saviour art thou.

ODE EIGHT
Heirmos

THE King of Heaven, Whom all the hosts of Angels hymn with their chants and praises of glory, praise ye and exalt Him to the ages for ever.

Most Holy Mother of God, save us.

DO not disdain those who seek the aid that thou dost grant, for, O Virgin Maiden, they do hymn thee, and they all exalt thee unto ages for ever.

Most Holy Mother of God, save us.

ON all who hymn thee with faith, O Virgin, and exalt thy truly ineffable Offspring, thou dost pour a great abundance of thy cures and healings.

Glory.

ALL the diseases that plague my soul dost thou make well, and the sufferings of the flesh thou healest also; wherefore, O thou Maiden full of grace, I glorify thee.

Both now.

ALL the assaultings of the temptations dost thou quell, and the onslaughts of the passions dost thou banish; wherefore do we hymn thee to all ages, O Virgin.

ODE NINE

Heirmos

Most rightly we confess thee as our God's Birthgiver, we who through thee have been saved, O thou Virgin most pure; with choirs of bodiless Angels, thee do we magnify.

Most Holy Mother of God, save us.

The torrent of my weeping spurn not with refusal, for thou didst give birth to Him Who doth take away all tears from every face, O thou Virgin, for He is Christ indeed.

Most Holy Mother of God, save us.

Do thou, O Virgin Maiden, fill my heart with gladness, for thou art she who received all the fulness of joy, and made to vanish away all sorrow of sinfulness.

Most Holy Mother of God, save us.

A haven and protection, and a wall unshaken, and a rejoicing and shelter and place of retreat do thou become, O thou Virgin, for those who flee to thee.

Glory.

Illumine with the radiance of thy light, O Virgin, all those who piously call thee the Mother of God; and do thou banish away all darkness of ignorance.

Both now.

BROUGHT low am I, O Virgin, in a place of sickness, and in a dwelling of anguish; grant healing to me, transforming all of my illness into full healthfulness.

And straightway:

IT is truly meet to call thee blest, the Theotokos, the ever-blessed and all-immaculate and Mother of our God. More honourable than the Cherubim, and beyond compare more glorious than the Seraphim, thee who without corruption gavest birth to God the Word, the very Theotokos, thee do we magnify.

The priest censeth the Holy Table and the people, or the house where the Canon is being chanted; and we chant the following Megalynaria:

HIGHER than the heavens above art thou, and thou art much purer than the radiance of the sun; for thou hast redeemed us out of the curse that held us. O Mistress of creation, with hymns we honour thee.

FROM the great abundance of all my sins, ill am I in body, ailing also am I in soul. Thee have I as refuge; do thou, therefore, help me, O hope of all the hopeless, for thou art full of grace.

O LADY and Mother of Christ our God, receive supplication from us wretches who beg of thee that thou make entreaty unto the One born from thee; O Mistress of creation, do thou intercede for us.

Now we chant with eagerness unto thee, with this ode most joyful, O all-hymned Mother of our God; together with the Baptist and all the saintly choirs, beseech, O Theotokos, that we find clemency.

SPEECHLESS be the lips of the impious who refuse to reverence thy revered icon which is known by the name Directress, and which hath been depicted for us by the Apostle Luke the Evangelist.

Then the Megalynarion of the Saint to whom the temple is dedicated.

Then:

O ALL ye arrays of Angelic Hosts, with the holy Baptist, the Apostles' twelve-numbered band, all the Saints together, as well as God's Birthgiver, pray make ye intercession for our deliverance.

The reader: Holy God. All-holy Trinity. Our Father.

The priest: For Thine is the kingdom, and the power, and the glory, of the Father, and of the

Son, and of the Holy Spirit, now and ever, and unto the ages of ages.

The reader: Amen. *But if there be no priest, then the reader:* Through the prayers of our holy Fathers, Lord Jesus Christ our God, have mercy on us. Amen.

Then we chant the following Troparia:
Plagal of Second Tone

HAVE mercy on us, Lord, have mercy on us; for lacking as we are in all defence, this supplication do we sinners offer unto Thee, as our Master: Have mercy on us.

Glory.

LORD, have mercy on us; for in Thee have we placed all our trust; be not wroth with us greatly, nor do Thou remember our iniquities; but look upon us even now, since Thou art compassionate, and do Thou redeem us from our enemies; for Thou art our God, and we Thy people; all are the works of Thy hands, and upon Thy Name have we called.

Both now. *Theotokion*

DO thou open the portal of compassion unto us, O most blessed Theotokos; for hoping in thee, let us not fail, we pray; through thee may we be delivered from adversities; for thou art the salvation of the Christian race.

And the priest, having again commemorated the faithful for whom the Canon is being chanted, maketh the dismissal.

After this, as the faithful kiss the icon of the Mother of God, the following Troparia are chanted with prostrations:

Second Tone. When he took Thee

ALL those who with faith flee unto thee, with thy mighty hand dost thou shelter, O pure one, as thou art good; no one else have we who sin as a perpetual intercessor for us with God in dangers and sorrows, we who have been burdened down with our abundant sins, Mother of God in the highest. Wherefore, we all fall down before thee; rescue us, thy servants from adversities.

Likewise:

JOY of all that sorrow art thou, and of the oppressed a protectress, and nurture of all the poor, comfort unto the estranged, a staff art thou of the blind, visitation of all the sick, a shelter and succour unto those brought down by pain, helper of orphaned ones: Mother of God in the highest art thou, O immaculate Maiden; hasten, we beseech thee, to redeem thy slaves.

Plagal of Fourth Tone

LADY, do thou receive the supplications of thy slaves, and deliver us from every affliction and necessity.

Second Tone

UNTO thee do I commit mine every hope, O Mother of God; guard me under thy shelter.

But during the Fast of the Mother of God, from the first to the fourteenth of August, the Exapostilaria at the conclusion of the Great Supplicatory Canon to the Theotokos (page 316) are chanted in place of the foregoing Troparia.

The priest: Through the prayers of our holy Fathers, Lord Jesus Christ our God, have mercy on us.

The choir: Amen.

THE SERVICE OF THE GREAT SUPPLICATORY CANON TO THE MOST HOLY THEOTOKOS

A Composition
of Emperor Theodore Ducas Lascaris

The Great Supplicatory Canon is chanted during the first fourteen days of August (that is, the Fast of the Mother of God), alternately with the Small Supplicatory Canon.

The priest: Blessed is our God, always, now and ever, and unto the ages of ages.

The reader: Amen. *And the introductory prayers, psalms, and hymns, as at the beginning of the Small Supplicatory Canon (pages 265–271).*

Then we chant the Canon, in Plagal of Fourth Tone:

ODE ONE
Heirmos

THE charioteer of Pharaoh was sunk in olden times by Moses's rod, which wrought a mighty wonder when, in the Cross's form, it struck the sea, dividing it in twain; and it led into safety sojourning Israel that fled by foot, chanting to the Lord God a song of praise.

Most Holy Mother of God, save us.

My humble soul is troubled by the rising tempests of afflictions and woes; and clouds of misfortunes overcome me, bringing darkness to my heart, O Bride of God. But since thou art the Mother of the Divine and Eternal Light, shine thy gladsome light and illumine me.

Most Holy Mother of God, save us.

From countless trials and afflictions, grievous woes, and from misfortunes of life have I been delivered by thy mighty strength, O spotless and immaculate Maid. I extol and I magnify thine immeasurable sympathy, and the loving care that thou hast for me.

Glory.

Having my hope now in thy mighty help, O Maid, I flee for refuge to thee; and unto thy shelter have I run wholeheartedly, O Lady, and I bow my knee; and I mourn and cry weeping: Do not disdain me, the wretched one, for thou art the refuge of Christian folk.

Both now.

I SHALL not cease from making known most manifestly thy great deeds, Maid of God; for if thou wert not present to intercede in my behalf and importune thy Son and God, who would free and deliver me from such tempests and turbulence, and surmount the perils that trouble me?

P RESERVE and save, O Theotokos, thy servants from every danger; after God do all of us for refuge flee unto thee; a firm rampart art thou and our protection.

I N thy good will, look thou on me, O all-hymned Theotokos; and do thou behold my body's grievous infirmity, and heal thou the cause of my soul's sorrow.

ODE THREE
Heirmos

O F the vault of the heavens art Thou, O Lord, Fashioner; so, too, of the Church art Thou founder; do Thou establish me in unfeigned love for Thee, Who art the height of things sought for, and staff of the faithful, O Thou only Friend of man.

Most Holy Mother of God, save us.

A T a loss and despairing, I cry with pain unto thee: Hasten, O thou fervent protection;

grant thou thy help to me, who am thy lowly slave and wretched servant, O Maiden; for with heartfelt fervour I come seeking for thine aid.

Most Holy Mother of God, save us.

Thou, O Lady, hast truly been shown to be wondrous now in thy benefactions and mercies granted to me, O Maid; hence do I glorify and acclaim thee, whilst praising thy great loving care and thy boundless solicitude.

Glory.

Mighty storms of misfortunes, O Lady, pass over me; and the swelling waves of afflictions plunge me into the depths. Make haste, O Full of Grace; lend me thy helping hand quickly, for thou art my fervent protectress and sure support.

Both now.

I profess thee, O Lady, as the true Mother of God: thee, who hast both banished and triumphed over the might of death; for as the source of Life, thou hast freed me from Hades' bonds, raising me to life, though to earth was I fallen down.

Preserve and save, O Theotokos, thy servants from every danger; after God do all of us for refuge flee unto thee; a firm rampart art thou and our protection.

In thy good will, look thou on me, O all-hymned Theotokos; and do thou behold my body's grievous infirmity, and heal thou the cause of my soul's sorrow.

Then the Priest commemorateth those for whom the Supplication is chanted:

Have mercy on us, O God, according to Thy great mercy, we pray Thee, hearken and have mercy.

The choir, after each petition:
Lord, have mercy. (3)

Again we pray for pious and Orthodox Christians.

Again we pray for our Bishop (*Name*), and for all our brotherhood (*or* sisterhood) in Christ.

Again we pray for mercy, life, peace, health, salvation, visitation, pardon and remission of the sins of the servants of God, all pious and Orthodox Christians who dwell and sojourn in this city, the parishioners and benefactors of this holy temple, and all that serve, chant, labour and gather herein; and for the servants of God (*Names*), and for the forgiveness of their every transgression, both voluntary and involuntary.

For a merciful and man-befriending God art Thou, and unto Thee do we send up glory, to the Father, and to the Son, and to the Holy Spirit, now and ever, and unto the ages of ages.

The choir: Amen.

After these petitions, we chant the following Sessional Hymn:

Second Tone

O FERVENT advocate, invincible battlement, fountain of mercy, and sheltering retreat for the world, earnestly we cry to thee: Lady Mother of God, hasten thou, and save us from all imperilment; for thou alone art our speedy protectress.

ODE FOUR
Heirmos

THOU art my strength; Thou art my power and might, O Lord; Thou art my God; Thou Who wast not absent from Thy Father's arms, Thou, Lord, art my joy. Thou hast deigned to visit our lowliness and our poverty. To Thee, therefore, I cry out with Abbacum the Prophet: Glory be to Thy power, O Friend of man.

Most Holy Mother of God, save us.

WHERE else shall I find me another to be my help? To what refuge shall I hasten to be saved? Whose fervent aid shall I have in need? Alas, I am shaken by life's affliction and turbulence. In thee alone, O Maiden, do I hope, trust, and glory; and I run to thy shelter; do thou save me.

Most Holy Mother of God, save us.

I MAGNIFY and I proclaim, O thou all-pure one, the sweet river of thy tender mercy and thy loving care; for with many gifts hath it greatly refreshed my tormented and truly lowly soul, afire in a furnace of misfortunes and sorrows; and I run to thy shelter; do thou save me.

Glory.

THOU, O pure Maid, all-holy Virgin and spotless one, art mine only steadfast shelter and retreat, and mighty wall that cannot be breached, my weapon of salvation. Do not disdain me, the prodigal, O hope of the despairing, and ally of the ailing, O thou gladness and help of afflicted ones.

Both now.

HOW shall I laud, how shall I worthily sing the praise, of thy boundless mercies and compassions which have ever cooled and refreshed my soul, aflame and tormented, O Lady, and wounded grievously? Indeed thy benefactions and thy providence, Maiden, are bestowed upon me most abundantly.

Preserve and save, O Theotokos, thy servants from every danger; after God do all of us for refuge flee unto thee; a firm rampart art thou and our protection.

In thy good will, look thou on me, O all-hymned Theotokos; and do thou behold my body's grievous infirmity, and heal thou the cause of my soul's sorrow.

ODE FIVE
Heirmos

Wherefore hast Thou deprived me, and cast me, the hapless one, far from Thy countenance? and the outer darkness hath enshrouded and cast its gloom over me. Yet, now I beseech Thee: Do Thou convert me and direct me to the light of Thy precepts, O Lord my God.

Most Holy Mother of God, save us.

As one grateful I cry out: Rejoice, O Virgin Mother; rejoice, O thou Bride of God; rejoice, O holy shelter; rejoice, O weapon and rampart invincible; rejoice, thou the protection and the assistance and salvation of all them that run to thee, O Maid of God.

Most Holy Mother of God, save us.

They that hate me without cause have made ready a dart and a sword and pit for me;

and my hapless body do they seek to destroy and to rend in twain; and they seek to bring me into the depths of earth, O pure one; but be quick and come save me from them, O Maid.

Glory.

FROM all need and affliction and from all disease and harm do thou deliver me; and by thy power, in thy shelter preserve me unwounded, Maid; and from every peril and foes that hate and war against me do thou hasten to save me, O all-hymned one.

Both now.

WHAT gift of thanksgiving shall I offer in gratefulness unto thee, O Maid, for thy boundless goodness and the favours and gifts that I have from thee? Hence, indeed I praise thee, and glorify and magnify thine inexpressible sympathy shown to me.

PRESERVE and save, O Theotokos, thy servants from every danger; after God do all of us for refuge flee unto thee; a firm rampart art thou and our protection.

IN thy good will, look thou on me, O all-hymned Theotokos; and do thou behold my body's grievous infirmity, and heal thou the cause of my soul's sorrow.

ODE SIX
Heirmos

ENTREATY do I pour forth unto the Lord, and to Him do I proclaim all my sorrows, for many woes fill my heart to repletion, and lo, my life unto Hades hath now drawn nigh; like Jonas do I pray to Thee: Raise me up from corruption, O Lord my God.

Most Holy Mother of God, save us.

THE storm clouds of grievous sorrows and distress shroud my hapless heart and soul in affliction, and with their gloom have they filled me, O Virgin. Yet since thou barest the Light Unapproachable, be quick to drive them far from me with the breeze of thy holy entreaties, Maid.

Most Holy Mother of God, save us.

A COMFORT art thou to me in my distress, and I have thee as a healer of all illness; of death art thou the most perfect destruction; thou art an unfailing fountain flowing with life, and speedy help and quick support of all them that are found in adversities.

Glory.

I SHALL not conceal the ever-flowing spring of the sympathy thou hast for me, O Lady, nor the abyss of thine infinite mercy, nor yet the fountain of thy boundless miracles; but unto all do I cry out and confess and declare and proclaim thy grace.

Both now.

THE turmoils of this life encircle me like unto bees about a honeycomb, O Virgin, and they have seized and now hold my heart captive, and I am pierced with the stings of afflictions, Maid; yet be thou, O all-holy one, my defender and helper and rescuer.

PRESERVE and save, O Theotokos, thy servants from every danger; after God do all of us for refuge flee unto thee; a firm rampart art thou and our protection.

IN thy good will, look thou on me, O all-hymned Theotokos; and do thou behold my body's grievous infirmity, and heal thou the cause of my soul's sorrow.

The priest maketh commemoration as before.

After the petitions, we chant the Kontakion, in Second Tone:

O PROTECTION of Christians that cannot be put to shame, mediation unto the Creator most constant: O despise not the suppliant voices of those who have sinned; but be thou quick, O good one, to come unto our aid, who in faith cry unto thee: Hasten to intercession, and speed thou to make supplication, thou who dost ever protect, O Theotokos, them that honour thee.

Then we chant the First Antiphon of the Hymns of Ascent of Fourth Tone:

FROM my youth do many passions war against me; but do Thou Thyself defend and save me, O my Saviour. (2)

YE haters of Sion shall be shamed by the Lord; for, like grass, by the fire shall ye be withered. (2)

Glory.

IN the Holy Spirit every soul is quickened, and through cleansing is exalted and made radiant by the Triple Unity in a hidden sacred manner.

Both now.

BY the Holy Spirit the streams of grace gush forth, watering all creation for the begetting of life.

And straightway we chant the Prokeimenon:

I shall commemorate thy name in every generation and generation. (2)

Verse: Hearken, O daughter, and see, and incline thine ear; and forget thine own people, and thy father's house; and the King shall greatly desire thy beauty.

And we chant the Prokeimenon once again.

The priest: And that we may be deemed worthy to hear the holy Gospel, let us beseech the Lord our God.

The choir: Lord, have mercy. (3)

The priest: Wisdom. Upright. Let us hear the holy Gospel. Peace be unto all.

The choir: And to thy spirit.

The priest: The reading is from the holy Gospel according to Saint Luke.

The choir: Glory to Thee, O Lord, glory to Thee.

The priest: Let us attend.

(Luke 10:38–42; 11:27–28)

At that time, Jesus entered into a certain village; and a certain woman named Martha received Him into her house. And she had a sister called Mary, which also sat at Jesus' feet, and heard His word. But Martha was distracted about much serving, and came to Him, and said: Lord, dost Thou not care that my sister hath left me to serve alone? Bid her therefore that she help me. And Jesus answered and said unto her: Martha, Martha, thou art anxious and troubled about many things; but one thing is needful; and Mary hath chosen the good part, which shall not be taken away from her. And it came to pass, as He spake these things, a certain woman from the multitude lifted up her voice, and said unto Him: Blessed is the womb that bare Thee, and the breasts which Thou hast sucked. And He said: Yea, verily, blessed are they that hear the word of God, and keep it.

The choir: Glory to Thee, O Lord, glory to Thee.

Glory. *Second Tone*

O Father, Word, and Spirit, the Trinity in Unity: blot out the multitude of mine offences.

Both now. *Theotokion*

By the intercessions of the Theotokos, O Merciful One, blot out the multitude of mine offences.

Verse: Have mercy on me, O God, according to Thy great mercy; and according to the multitude of Thy compassions blot out my transgression.

Plagal of Second Tone. Having laid up all their hope

O ENTRUST me not, I pray, to any human protection, O our Lady, holy one, but do thou accept the prayer of thy supplicant. Sorrow hath fettered me, and I am unable to endure and bear the demons' darts; a shelter have I not, neither place to run, I, the wretched one; embattled from all sides am I, and no consolation have I but thee. Mistress of creation, protection and hope of faithful ones: Turn not away when I pray to thee; do that which will profit me.

Theotokia

FROM thee is no one turned away ashamed and empty who doth run to thee for refuge, O pure Virgin Theotokos; but he asketh the favour and receiveth the gift from thee, unto the profit of his own request.

THE transformation of the afflicted and the relief of those in sickness art thou in truth, O Virgin Theotokos; save thy people and thy flock, thou who art the peace of the embattled, and who art the calm of the storm-driven, the only protectress of those who believe.

Then the prayer of the priest, Save, O God, Thy people ... *with the responses of the choir and the concluding exclamation of the priest, as in the Small Supplicatory Canon (pages 283–284).*

And we complete the remaining Odes of the Canon:

ODE SEVEN
Heirmos

THE Three Hebrew Children in the furnace trampled on the flames with courage and great boldness; they turned fire to dew, and cried out with a great voice: Blessed art Thou, O Lord our God, unto ages of ages.

Most Holy Mother of God, save us.

ILLUMINE my way, for I am darkened by the night of many sins, O Theotokos; thou hast brought forth the Light, and art in truth the blameless and undefiled vessel of light; hence with love do I praise thee.

Most Holy Mother of God, save us.

BE thou my shelter and protection and my help and boast, O Virgin Theotokos; of all manner of help have I now been stripped naked, O strength of those bereft of help, and thou hope of those without hope.

Glory.

WITH my whole soul and understanding and with all my heart and with my lips I praise thee, having truly enjoyed thy many benefactions; yet boundless are thy miracles, and thy goodness is unending.

Both now.

LOOK thou with graciousness upon me, and dispel the evil plight that doth beset me; and from grievous distress and harm and temptations and perils do thou rescue me in thine infinite mercy.

PRESERVE and save, O Theotokos, thy servants from every danger; after God do all of us for refuge flee unto thee; a firm rampart art thou and our protection.

IN thy good will, look thou on me, O all-hymned Theotokos; and do thou behold my body's grievous infirmity, and heal thou the cause of my soul's sorrow.

ODE EIGHT
Heirmos

LET us ever extol and praise the Lord God Who was seen of old on the holy mount in glory, Who by the fiery bush revealed the great mystery of the Ever-virgin and undefiled Maiden unto the Prophet Moses.

Most Holy Mother of God, save us.

BE thou moved to compassion, O Virgin, and disdain me not, for life's tempests overwhelm me. But be thou quick, O modest one, and lend me thy helping hand, O Maiden, for I perish drowning engulfed by life's misfortunes.

Most Holy Mother of God, save us.

TIMES of sorrows, necessity, and trouble, and misfortunes in life have found me, O pure Maiden; and from all sides temptations have encircled me; but be thou mine ally, and do thou protect me in thine almighty shelter.

Glory.

IN distress, I have thee, Maid, as my haven, and in sorrows and griefs thou art my joy and gladness; and in all illness, thou hast been my quick help, and rescuer in perils, and in all temptations my guardian and protectress.

Both now.

REJOICE, fiery throne of the Lord God; rejoice, thou sacred vessel that art filled with manna; rejoice, thou golden lampstand and unquenchable lamp; rejoice, O glory of virgins and thou boast and adornment of mothers.

PRESERVE and save, O Theotokos, thy servants from every danger; after God do all of us for refuge flee unto thee; a firm rampart art thou and our protection.

IN thy good will, look thou on me, O all-hymned Theotokos; and do thou behold my body's grievous infirmity, and heal thou the cause of my soul's sorrow.

ODE NINE
Heirmos

THE heavens were astonished and stood in awe, and the ends of the earth, Maid, were sore amazed, for God appeared bodily to mankind as very man. And lo, thy womb hath proved to be vaster and more spacious than heaven's heights. For this, O Theotokos, the choirs and assemblies of men and Angels magnify thy name.

Most Holy Mother of God, save us.

TO whom else shall I flee, O thou Maid most pure, and to whom shall I run for help and be saved? Where shall I go, and where shall I find me a safe retreat? Whose warm protection shall I have? Who shall be a helper in my distress? In thee alone I hope, Maid; in thee alone I glory; and trusting in thee, I have fled to thee.

Most Holy Mother of God, save us.

TO number thy great deeds and thy mighty acts is not possible for man, O Bride of God, nor yet can one tell of the unfathomable abyss of thine unending miracles that surpass all knowledge, and which are wrought for those that venerate thee and honour thee with longing as the true Mother of our Lord and God.

Glory.

WITH anthems of thanksgiving I glorify and chant praise to thine infinite mercy, and thy boundless might I confess unceasingly unto all; and with my soul and heart and mind and my lips I magnify and proclaim the many benefactions that thou hast poured upon me in thy compassion, O thou Bride of God.

Both now.

ACCEPT thou mine entreaty and my poor prayer, and disdain not my weeping and sighs, O Maid, nor my lament, but be quick to help me since thou art good. Do thou fulfil mine every plea; thou canst do this in that thou broughtest forth our mighty God and Master, if thou but look upon me and bow down to mine utter lowliness.

PRESERVE and save, O Theotokos, thy servants from every danger; after God do all of us for refuge flee unto thee; a firm rampart art thou and our protection.

IN thy good will, look thou on me, O all-hymned Theotokos; and do thou behold my body's grievous infirmity, and heal thou the cause of my soul's sorrow.

And straightway:

IT is truly meet to call thee blest, the Theotokos, the ever-blessed and all-immaculate and Mother of our God. More honourable than the Cherubim, and beyond compare more glorious than the Seraphim, thee who without corruption gavest birth to God the Word, the very Theotokos, thee do we magnify.

The priest censeth the Holy Table and the people, or the house where the Canon is being chanted; and we chant the following Megalynaria:

HIGHER than the heavens above art thou, and thou art much purer than the radiance of the sun; for thou hast redeemed us out of the curse that held us. O Mistress of creation, with hymns we honour thee.

FROM the great abundance of all my sins, ill am I in body, ailing also am I in soul. Thee have I as refuge; do thou, therefore, help me, O hope of all the hopeless, for thou art full of grace.

O LADY and Mother of Christ our God, receive supplication from us wretches who beg of thee that thou make entreaty unto the One born from thee; O Mistress of creation, do thou intercede for us.

Now we chant with eagerness unto thee, with this ode most joyful, O all-hymned Mother of our God; together with the Baptist and all the saintly choirs, beseech, O Theotokos, that we find clemency.

Speechless be the lips of the impious who refuse to reverence thy revered icon which is known by the name Directress, and which hath been depicted for us by the Apostle Luke the Evangelist.

Then the Megalynarion of the Saint to whom the church is dedicated.

Then:

O all ye arrays of Angelic Hosts, with the holy Baptist, the Apostles' twelve-numbered band, all the Saints together, as well as God's Birthgiver, pray make ye intercession for our deliverance.

The reader: Holy God. All-holy Trinity. Our Father.

The priest: For Thine is the kingdom, and the power, and the glory, of the Father, and of the Son, and of the Holy Spirit, now and ever, and unto the ages of ages.

The reader: Amen. *But if there be no priest, then the reader:* Through the prayers of our holy Fathers,

Lord Jesus Christ our God, have mercy on us. Amen.

Then we chant the following Troparia:
Plagal of Second Tone

HAVE mercy on us, Lord, have mercy on us; for lacking as we are in all defence, this supplication do we sinners offer unto Thee, as our Master: Have mercy on us.

Glory.

LORD, have mercy on us; for in Thee have we placed all our trust; be not wroth with us greatly, nor do Thou remember our iniquities; but look upon us even now, since Thou art compassionate, and do Thou redeem us from our enemies; for Thou art our God, and we Thy people; all are the works of Thy hands, and upon Thy Name have we called.

Both now. Theotokion

DO thou open the portal of compassion unto us, O most blessed Theotokos; for hoping in thee, let us not fail, we pray; through thee may we be delivered from adversities; for thou art the salvation of the Christian race.

And the priest, having again commemorated the faithful for whom the Canon is being chanted, maketh the dismissal.

After this, as the faithful kiss the icon of the Mother of God, the following Exapostilaria are chanted with prostrations:

Third Tone

O YE Apostles from afar, being now gathered together here in the vale of Gethsemane, give burial to my body; and Thou, my Son and my God, receive Thou my spirit.

THOU art the sweetness of Angels, the gladness of afflicted ones, and the protectress of Christians, O Virgin Mother of our Lord; be thou my helper, and save me from out of eternal torments.

I HAVE thee as Mediatress with the man-befriending God; may He not censure my actions before the hosts of the Angels. I supplicate thee, O Virgin, come unto mine aid most quickly.

THOU art a gold-entwined tower and twelve-wall encircled city, a throne besprinkled with sunbeams, a royal chair of the King. O inexplicable wonder! that thou dost milk-feed the Master.

The priest: Through the prayers of our holy Fathers, Lord Jesus Christ our God, have mercy on us.

The choir: Amen.

ΜΡ ΘΥ

ΙϹ ΧϹ

Η ΠΕΛΑΓΟ-
ΝΙΤΙϹϹΑ

GUARDIAN ANGEL

TAKE
ME BY MY
WRETCHID
AND OUT
STRETCH-
ED HAND

A SUPPLICATORY CANON
TO THE
GUARDIAN ANGEL
OF A MAN'S LIFE

A Composition of the Monk
John Mauropus

Plagal of Fourth Tone
ODE ONE
Heirmos

TRAVERSING the water as on dry land, and thereby escaping from the toils of Egypt's land, the Israelites cried aloud, proclaiming: Unto our God and Redeemer let us now sing.

O holy Angel, my Guardian, intercede in my behalf.

O UNSLEEPING guardian of my soul, I now sing thy praises, thou protector of all my life; for thou art the guide that God assigned me, O thou divine Angel of the Almighty God.

O holy Angel, my Guardian, intercede in my behalf.

O WORD, Who wouldst have all us mortals saved, to Thy holy Angels hast Thou given charge over us, as guides and enlighteners of mankind, to lead us all by the hand unto fear of Thee.

O holy Angel, my Guardian, intercede in my behalf.

My guardian, protector, and faithful guide, the light of repentance do thou now cause to dawn in me; for I am held fast in gloomy darkness, and the black cloud of my passions hath shrouded me.

Glory.

A MURKY and vile flood of shameful thoughts doth well up within me, and doth sunder my mind from God. O thou who art my divine protector, come thou and make it to dry up for evermore.

Both now. *Theotokion*

O LADY, thou art the serenity, the calm and the haven of those stormbound on seas of sins; and therefore I flee unto thy haven, as divers passions do toss me upon their waves.

ODE THREE
Heirmos

OF the vault of the heavens art Thou, O Lord, Fashioner; so, too, of the Church art Thou founder; do Thou establish me in unfeigned love for Thee, Who art the height of things sought for, and staff of the faithful, O Thou only Friend of man.

O holy Angel, my Guardian, intercede in my behalf.

I AM nailed to things earthly, for I exist as the clod of an intermingling of lowly earth mixed with clay and dust; but, O my rescuer, my guide and mighty protector, turn mine aspiration to heavenly things above.

O holy Angel, my Guardian, intercede in my behalf.

I PROVOKE thee and grieve thee and fill thee with bitterness all the night and day with my wicked deeds and my trespasses; and so against thy will do I constrain and compel thee, who art my defender, to stand far away from me.

O holy Angel, my Guardian, intercede in my behalf.

I REMAIN unrepentant and uncorrected in life, and I am the cause of thy grief and heavy despondency; wherefore grant unto me that I repent with my whole heart and that I may gladden thee, O my good guardian.

Glory.

T HOU invisibly seest the face of God at all times, Who doth sit in Heaven and look upon earth noetically, making it tremble sore; O holy Angel, my guardian, ceaselessly entreat Him to set me among the saved.

Both now. *Theotokion*

M IND, volition, and reason have I as a gift of God, so that, recognizing my Lord, I honour Him with good works; but in dishonouring the gift because of my passions, I affront the Giver. O Lady, do thou save me.

SESSIONAL HYMN
Fourth Tone. Thou Who wast raised up

O GOOD protector of my soul and my body, my God-appointed and divine guardian Angel, in imitating God, do thou now overlook all the failings and the sins of my soul in its sufferings; rescue me from the diverse meshes of the deceiver; and make our God compassionate to me, that He may grant me forgiveness on judgment day.

ODE FOUR

Heirmos

THOU art my strength; Thou art my power and might, O Lord; Thou art my God; Thou Who wast not absent from Thy Father's arms, Thou, Lord, art my joy. Thou hast deigned to visit our lowliness and our poverty. To Thee, therefore, I cry out with Abbacum the Prophet: Glory be to Thy power, O Friend of man.

O holy Angel, my Guardian, intercede in my behalf.

I GIVE no thought unto that terrible judgment seat, O my Saviour, where I shall be haled to render strict account for all words and deeds; nor death's hidden hour do I ever bring to mind at all, remaining uncorrected. O my guide and mine Angel, I beseech thee: Do thou not abandon me.

O holy Angel, my Guardian, intercede in my behalf.

WITH care and zeal, I have performed every wickedness from my childhood; and with lawless words and deeds I have not ceased from provoking thee, mine own lifelong helper. Despond not, I pray thee, weary not; but even so persist thou in admonishing, teaching, and instructing and strengthening me to good.

O holy Angel, my Guardian, intercede in my behalf.

O IMITATE the great forbearance of God the Word, He that came to call unto repentance all us sinful men, and constraineth not, but loveth and seeketh amendment that cometh willingly; do thou, my guide, in likewise even now abide with me in forbearance and loving long-suffering.

Glory.

THOUGH sin had once taken me far from God, since I am an unworthy servant void of profit, yet in clemency and in tender love did Jesus my Master both take me again and make me His; but spurning this great favour of my Lord and Creator, O divine Angel, thee also do I grieve.

Both now. *Theotokion*

THE Lord is king, and truly reigneth eternally over a Kingdom that shall never fall away or come to nought; and as saith the psalms, from thee, God's pure Mother, is He clothed with fairest majesty, that holy flesh come from thee, in the which He hath slain death and destroyed all its kingdom and sovereignty.

ODE FIVE
Heirmos

WHEREFORE hast Thou deprived me, and cast me, the hapless one, far from Thy countenance? and the outer darkness hath enshrouded and cast its gloom over me. Yet, now I beseech Thee: Do Thou convert me and direct me to the light of Thy precepts, O Lord my God.

O holy Angel, my Guardian, intercede in my behalf.

I HAVE thee as my guardian, and my true companion that dwelleth close at my side, urging me to goodness, while attending me, walking the way with me, counselling salvation; how then shall I receive forgiveness, since despite all these things, I live senselessly?

O holy Angel, my Guardian, intercede in my behalf.

O MY mighty defender, standing with great boldness before the Almighty's throne, thou dost dance in gladness round the King of creation with angel-kind; wherefore, do thou pray Him that I be granted the forgiveness of my many transgressions and evil deeds.

O holy Angel, my Guardian, intercede in my behalf.

THOU foreseest the torments and the heavy punishments yonder awaiting me, grieving for my hardness and my blindness and unfeeling recklessness; and in tender mercy, thou sighest, gloomy, and dejected, filled with grief, O my faithful deliverer.

Glory.

NOT so much as an hour, even for a moment or for the least space of time, have I once allowed thee, my most kind benefactor and guardian, joy and exultation or jubilation over my goodness; for with sins do I ever corrupt myself.

Both now. Theotokion

HE Whom no mind can fathom hath appeared from thee as a babe, O all-blameless Maid, He that in His knowledge weighed the mountains and valleys as in a scale, and arrayed in beauty the choirs of stars, and ever stirreth both the dew of the morn and the breath of winds.

ODE SIX

Heirmos

ENTREATY do I pour forth unto the Lord, and to Him do I proclaim all my sorrows, for many woes fill my heart to repletion, and lo, my life unto Hades hath now drawn nigh; like Jonas do I pray to Thee: Raise me up from corruption, O Lord my God.

O holy Angel, my Guardian, intercede in my behalf.

D O not cease encamping round about my soul, daily guarding me from every affliction; but do thou check the wild raging of demons, and end their bestial assaults roused against my soul, O good protector sent by God, for in thee do I have a most fervent help.

O holy Angel, my Guardian, intercede in my behalf.

S INCE thou art sweet-smelling myrrh beyond all price, do thou not abominate my foul stinking; do not depart from thy servant for ever; be mine inseparable guardian perpetually; the sun itself is not defiled when it passeth through places defiled and foul.

O holy Angel, my Guardian, intercede in my behalf.

I MPLORE Him Who hath supported by a word His high chambers in the waters, to grant me the grace to rain floods of tears in great showers, that through my weeping, my heart might be purified and so may clearly see my God, O my guardian, who ever protectest me.

O holy Angel, my Guardian, intercede in my behalf.

O THOU who art immaterial and pure, immaterially now standing before God, the Immaterial and Pure One by nature, thou hast great closeness and audience with our Lord; beseech Him earnestly for me, that He grant me salvation of soul, I pray.

Glory.

MAY shame and confusion wholly cover up the deformed and foul and most gloomy faces of all my foes when my base soul is parted from its abased tabernacle formed out of clay; and with thy shining sacred wings, come and shelter it swiftly, O trusted guide.

Both now. *Theotokion*

MUCH higher than Seraphim and Cherubim and more holy than the all-holy Angels art thou, O Lady. Do thou therefore show forth my vile and grovelling mind to be far above the love of gross and earthly things; from the earth lift it up to celestial love.

KONTAKION
Second Tone. Thou soughtest the heights

O SERVANT of God, my guardian most excellent, for ever abide with me, the sinner most profane, and deliver me from the demons' every wickedness and deceit; guide me unto the godly paths that lead unto spotless and eternal life.

ODE SEVEN
Heirmos

ONCE from out of Judea did the Children go down to the land of Babylon; the fire of the furnace they trampled down while chanting by their faith in the Trinity: O God of our Fathers, blessed art Thou.

O holy Angel, my Guardian, intercede in my behalf.

O MY helper and succour, cease not driving off mightily with thy fiery sword the multitudes unnumbered of unseen thieves and robbers who assail me from every side in seeking to seize and mangle my soul.

O holy Angel, my Guardian, intercede in my behalf.

IN the dread day of judgment, when my God and my Judge shall condemn my sinful soul, who even ere that judgment am now condemned already by my conscience in very truth, forget not thy servant, O my good guide.

O holy Angel, my Guardian, intercede in my behalf.

HAVING matter as mother, clay as father, and dust as forefather, O my guide, I look to earth at all times by reason of the kinship; O protector, grant that I look on Heaven's high beauty freely some day.

O holy Angel, my Guardian, intercede in my behalf.

BEING comely in beauty, being sweet and most graceful, my guide, thou sunlike mind, stand joyously beside me with bright regard most cheerful and a smiling face in the hour when I shall be taken far from the earth.

Glory.

IN thy bowels of mercy, in the great and exceeding wealth of thy love for man, when I depart the body, protect me in the shelter of thy wings, that I might not see the hideous faces of the foul fiends.

Both now. *Theotokion*

O THOU heavenly portal, saving gateway, and ladder noetic and sublime, whereby our God descended, whereby we men ascended: In thy mercy grant me thy slave the Kingdom of Heaven, O modest Maid.

ODE EIGHT
Heirmos

THE Chaldee tyrant, mad with rage, fired his furnace of blazing flame seven times more hot against the worshippers of God; but seeing them kept in safety by a power greater than his, he then cried aloud: Ye children, bless the Creator, the Saviour and Redeemer; O ye priests, sing His praises; exalt Him, O ye people, to all the endless ages.

O holy Angel, my Guardian, intercede in my behalf.

I HAVE received thee from my God as a succour and champion, as a help and as my great defender after God, O all-holy Angel; wherefore cease not from admonishing me, from instructing me, from teaching me what I must do; and grant illumination to my mind without ceasing, till thou set me before Christ among the saved and blessed.

O holy Angel, my Guardian, intercede in my behalf.

ON that dread day when thrones are set and the Ancient of Days shall sit, when the books are opened and all things shall be revealed, when men shall be judged and all the earth shall quake with terrible fear, and all things that be, shall sorely shudder and tremble, then show thy love for mankind in me, O my protector, and by thy prayers to Christ God, redeem me from Gehenna.

O holy Angel, my Guardian, intercede in my behalf.

LIKE cunning foxes full of guile, and like ravenous birds of prey, do the pestilential demons, hateful unto God, invisibly compass me like unto bees that swarm round a hive;

like blood-thirsty fowl that eat the flesh of the fallen, they all fly round about me. O my God-given guardian, come shelter me at once, as an eagle doth its nestlings.

O holy Angel, my Guardian, intercede in my behalf.

GRANT me great floods of tears that flow from mine eyelids in endless streams, a profuse outpouring washing me from head to foot; that, wearing a garment of repentance rendered whiter than snow, I be wholly cleansed and rid of every defilement, that I may enter into the divine bridal chamber while honouring thee with praises, my helper and defender.

O holy Angel, my Guardian, intercede in my behalf.

WITH passions I have made my heart an abode for noetic swine, though it is the temple of my Christ, Who fashioned me; O help of my soul, I pray thee, give me strength to cleanse it anew, with the myrrh of prayers and godly purity's balsam to sprinkle it and cense it, that again and for ever it might become the sweet-smelling temple of Christ Jesus.

Glory.

MY guide and my deliverer, my protector and guardian, O thou overseer of my lost and desperate soul, when I shall be raised from earth for judgment by the trumpet's dread blast, then, I pray thee, come and, being gladsome and gracious, stand at my side and help me, O my faithful protector, and take my fear away by the hope of my salvation.

Both now. *Theotokion*

OF all my goods, no need hast thou, who ineffably didst conceive the Bestower of all good, the Saviour of the world; and since I have nothing worthy of thy mercy, O Full of Grace, in thy boundless love and in the superabundance of thine exceeding kindness, freely have mercy on me, for thou hast given birth to the Fountain of compassion.

ODE NINE
Heirmos

TERROR filled every ear that learned the unheard-of condescension of God the Word: how of His own good will the Lord Most High came down to such lowliness as from a virgin's womb to take a body, becoming man; hence, we the faithful flock magnify the undefiled Mother of our God.

O holy Angel, my Guardian, intercede in my behalf.

O MY protector and my help, when my spirit shall be forcibly rent from me,

would that I then behold thee standing glad
and radiant and serene upon the right hand of
my poor and utterly wretched soul and driving
far away all my bitter foes who seek to lay hold
on me.

O holy Angel, my Guardian, intercede in my behalf.

As the divine servant of God, who perform-
est His divine will, thou dost abound in
boldness at His throne; O holy Angel, for this
cause fervently entreat and plead with Him
for me, that I, being saved through thee, may
ever sing the praise of thy great protection
and shelter over me.

O holy Angel, my Guardian, intercede in my behalf.

All of my life have I misspent in much van-
ity and unfruitful idleness, and I am nigh
the end; I pray thee, O my guardian and my
guide, be thou my strong defender and invincible champion when I shall have to pass
through the grim exactors of this world's
wicked prince.

O holy Angel, my Guardian, intercede in my behalf.

O my protector, never cease to turn all the
deviations, the wanderings, the base captivity and foulness of my mind, the obscenity
of mine unclean and filthy thoughts to virtuous

purposes and unto goodly thoughts, and beget in me compunction like fervent fire.

O holy Angel, my Guardian, intercede in my behalf.

IN Thy compassion, overcome the unnumbered multitude of mine evils, O Only-begotten and transcendently good Jesus, through the divine entreaties of Thy hallowed immaterial minister, whom Thou, as Friend of man, sentest me as guardian when I was yet a babe.

Glory.

SINCE, after God Most High Himself, I have placed all of my hope of salvation in thee, my good guardian, my helper and protector, I pray of thee: Take all the Angels' choirs as fellow helpers and advocates, and making common plea, intercede with God unceasingly for my sake.

Both now. *Theotokion*

THOU who hast given birth to God, overthrow the proud barbarians' arrogance and lift aloft the horn of them that cleave to piety; and do thou preserve from tyranny and siege of foes this, thy flock, wherein thy great and glorious name is magnified and glorified faithfully.

And the following Stichera:
Second Tone. O house of Ephratha

O ANGEL of our God, cease not to make entreaty for me, thy lowly servant, as thou dost stand with boldness before the Holy Trinity.

H AVING received from God the might to guard my poor soul, cease never to protect it, but do thou ever shelter it in the shelter of thy wings.

T HANKS be to Jesus Christ, Who gave thee to me freely to be my soul's great guardian and weapon 'gainst my foes, O thou Angel honoured by our God.

G RANT thou that even I attain unto the Kingdom of Christ our God, the Most High, that with thee I may cry out the awesome and thrice-holy hymn.

B EING a second light that after God doth shine forth, O guardian, cease not caring for me, that even I see the triply-shining Godhead's light.

Glory; both now. *Theotokion*

O SOVEREIGN Lady of the Angels and us mortals, most holy Theotokos, cease not to pray thy Son for thy servant's sake, O Virgin Maid.

A PRAYER
TO THE GUARDIAN ANGEL

O HOLY Angel, attendant of my wretched soul and of mine afflicted life, forsake me not, a sinner, neither depart from me for mine incontinency. Give no place to the evil demon to subdue me with the oppression of this mortal body; but take me by my wretched and outstretched hand, and lead me in the way of salvation. Yea, O holy Angel of God, the guardian and protector of my hapless soul and body, forgive me all things whatsoever wherewith I have troubled thee, all the days of my life, and if I have sinned in anything this day. Shelter me in this present night, and keep me from every affront of the enemy, lest I anger God by any sin; and intercede with the Lord in my behalf, that He might strengthen me in the fear of Him, and make me a worthy servant of His goodness. Amen.

ΠΊΕΤΕ ἐξ   ☩   ἀυτῦ πάν
τες

DRINK YE ALL OF IT

THE SERVICE
OF PREPARATION FOR
HOLY COMMUNION

When thou art preparing to receive the Immaculate Mysteries, first read the Service of Small Compline to the end of the Creed (pages 31–38), and then say the following Canon with compunction:

THE CANON OF PREPARATION
FOR HOLY COMMUNION

Second Tone

ODE ONE

Heirmos

COME, O ye people, let us sing a song unto Christ God, Who divided the sea, and made a way for the people which He had brought up out of the bondage of Egypt; for He is glorified.

Have mercy on me, O God, have mercy on me.

MAY Thy holy Body be for me the Bread of life everlasting, O compassionate Lord, and may Thy precious Blood be a remedy for diverse maladies.

Have mercy on me, O God, have mercy on me.

DEFILED by unseemly deeds, wretched as I am, I am unworthy, O Christ, to partake of Thine immaculate Body and divine Blood; but make me worthy of them.

Most Holy Mother of God, save us.

O BLESSED Bride of God, O good land which produced the Ear of Wheat which knew no husbandry and which bringeth salvation to the world: grant that I who eat thereof may be saved.

ODE THREE
Heirmos

UPON the rock of faith hast Thou now confirmed me; Thou hast enlarged my mouth over mine adversaries; my spirit hath rejoiced mightily in chanting: There is none holy as our most holy God, and there is none righteous but Thee, O Lord Most High.

Have mercy on me, O God, have mercy on me.

GRANT me, O Christ, teardrops to cleanse the defilement of my heart, that, purified and with a good conscience, I may draw nigh with fear and faith, O Master, to the communion of Thy divine Gifts.

Have mercy on me, O God, have mercy on me.

MAY Thine immaculate Body and divine Blood be for the forgiveness of mine offences, for communion with the Holy Spirit, and for life everlasting, O Friend of man, and for estrangement from passions and sorrows.

Most Holy Mother of God, save us.

O ALL-HOLY one, table of the Bread of Life which for mercy's sake came down from on high and gave new life to the world, make even me, who am unworthy, worthy now with fear to taste thereof and live.

ODE FOUR
Heirmos

NEITHER an angel, nor yet an ambassador, O my Lord, but Thyself incarnate camest from a Virgin and holy Maid, rescuing me, the whole man. Wherefore, I cry to Thee: Glory to Thy power, O Lord my God.

Have mercy on me, O God, have mercy on me.

O MOST Merciful One, Who wast incarnate for us, Thou didst will to be slain as a sheep for the sins of mortals. Wherefore also, I implore Thee to blot out mine offences.

Have mercy on me, O God, have mercy on me.

HEAL the wounds of my soul, O Lord, and wholly sanctify me, the wretched one, and make me worthy, O Master, to partake of Thy divine Mystical Supper.

Most Holy Mother of God, save us.

Make Him Who came forth from thy womb, O Lady, to be gracious also unto me; and keep me, thy suppliant, blameless and free of stain, that, by receiving within me the noetic Pearl, I may be sanctified.

ODE FIVE
Heirmos

O Lord, Thou Bestower of light and Creator of the ages, guide us in the light of Thy commandments; for we know none other God than Thee.

Have mercy on me, O God, have mercy on me.

As Thou didst foretell, O Christ, so let it be even now to Thine abject slave, and abide in me as Thou didst promise; for behold, I eat Thy divine Body and drink Thy Blood.

Have mercy on me, O God, have mercy on me.

O Word of God, and God, may the live coal of Thy Body be for the enlightenment of me who am darkened, and may Thy Blood be for the cleansing of my defiled soul.

Most Holy Mother of God, save us.

O MARY, thou Mother of God, august tabernacle of the Sweet Fragrance: by thy prayers, make me a chosen vessel, that I may partake of the holy Gifts of thy Child.

ODE SIX
Heirmos

C OMPASSED by the abyss of my many sins, I invoke the boundless abyss and unfathomed deep of Thy compassion, O my Christ: Raise me out of corruption, O Lord my God.

Have mercy on me, O God, have mercy on me.

O SAVIOUR, sanctify my mind, soul, heart, and body; and grant that without condemnation, O Master, I may approach the dread Mysteries.

Have mercy on me, O God, have mercy on me.

G RANT me estrangement from passions, and the increase of Thy grace, and assurance of life by my participation in Thy holy Mysteries, O Christ.

Most Holy Mother of God, save us.

O HOLY Word of God, and God, as I now approach Thy divine Mysteries, sanctify the whole of me, by the supplications of Thy holy Mother.

KONTAKION
Second Tone

DISDAIN me not to receive now, O Christ, the Bread which is Thy Body, and Thy divine Blood, and to partake, O Master, of Thine immaculate and dread Mysteries; and may it not be unto me, the wretched one, for judgment, but for eternal and immortal life.

ODE SEVEN
Heirmos

IN Deira's great plain, where the golden image was shown adoration, Thy three courageous Youths despised the impious decree issued by the king. Cast into the flames, they were sprinkled with Thy dew and they cried in chant: Blessed art Thou, O Lord our God, even the God of our Fathers.

Have mercy on me, O God, have mercy on me.

MAY the reception of Thine immortal Mysteries, the Source of every good, O Christ, be now unto me light, and life, and dispassion, and the cause of furtherance and proficiency in divine virtue, O only Good One, that I may glorify Thee.

Have mercy on me, O God, have mercy on me.

THAT I may be redeemed from passions, enemies, want, and every affliction, I now draw nigh with trembling, love, and reverence to Thine immortal and divine Mysteries, O Friend of man, and chant unto Thee: Blessed art Thou, the God of our Fathers.

Most Holy Mother of God, save us.

O THOU who art graced of God, and gavest birth incomprehensibly to Christ the Saviour, I thy slave, impure as I am, now beseech thee, the pure one: From all defilement of flesh and spirit do thou cleanse me who am now about to approach the immaculate Mysteries.

ODE EIGHT
Heirmos

To the Lord God Who did descend to the Hebrew Children in the fiery furnace and did transform the flames and the burning heat into dew, chant praises and hymns, O all ye works of His, and exalt Him greatly to ages and all ages.

Have mercy on me, O God, have mercy on me.

GRANT me, who am despairing, to be a communicant now of Thy heavenly, dread, and holy Mysteries, O Christ, and of Thy Divine and Mystical Supper, O God my Saviour.

Have mercy on me, O God, have mercy on me.

I FLEE for refuge under Thy compassion, O Good One, and I cry to Thee with fear:

Abide in me, O Saviour, and I in Thee, as Thou didst say; for lo, trusting in Thy mercy, I eat Thy Body and drink Thy Blood.

Most Holy Mother of God, save us.

I TREMBLE as I receive the Fire, lest I should be burned as wax and as grass. O dread mystery! O divine compassion! How is it that I who am but clay partake of the divine Body and Blood and am made incorruptible?

ODE NINE
Heirmos

OUR God and Lord, the Son of the Father which is without beginning, hath appeared to us incarnate of a Virgin, to enlighten those in darkness, and to gather the dispersed; wherefore we magnify the all-hymned Theotokos.

Have mercy on me, O God, have mercy on me.

THE Lord is good: O taste and see! For of old He became like unto us for our sake, and offered Himself once as an offering to His Father, and is ever slain, sanctifying them that partake of Him.

Have mercy on me, O God, have mercy on me.

MAY I be sanctified in body and soul, O Master; may I be enlightened; may I be saved; may I become Thy dwelling-place by the communion of the sacred Mysteries, having Thee with the Father and the Spirit abiding in me, O most merciful Benefactor.

Glory.

MAY Thy most precious Body and Blood be to me as fire and light, O my Saviour, consuming the substance of sin and burning the thorns of my passions, and enlightening the whole of me to worship Thy Divinity.

Both now.

GOD took flesh of thy pure blood. Wherefore, every generation doth hymn thee, O Lady, and the multitudes of the noetic beings glorify thee; for through thee we have clearly seen the Master of all, Who assumed the nature of man.

And we complete the Service of Small Compline:

IT is truly meet to call thee blest, the Theotokos, the ever-blessed and all-immaculate and Mother of our God. More honourable than the Cherubim, and beyond compare more glorious than the Seraphim, thee who without corruption gavest birth to God the Word, the very Theotokos, thee do we magnify.

Then:

Holy God. All-holy Trinity. Our Father.

Through the prayers of our holy Fathers, Lord Jesus Christ our God, have mercy on us. Amen.

And the following Troparion:

WHEN the glorious disciples were enlightened at the washing of the feet, then Judas the ungodly one was stricken and darkened with the love of silver. And unto the lawless judges did he deliver Thee, the righteous Judge. O thou lover of money, behold thou him who for the sake thereof did hang himself; flee from that insatiable soul that dared such things against the Master. O Thou Who art good unto all, Lord, glory be to Thee.

Lord, have mercy. (40)

Then read the prayer: Thou Who at all times and at every hour ... *and the rest of the Service of Small Compline (pages 40–45).*

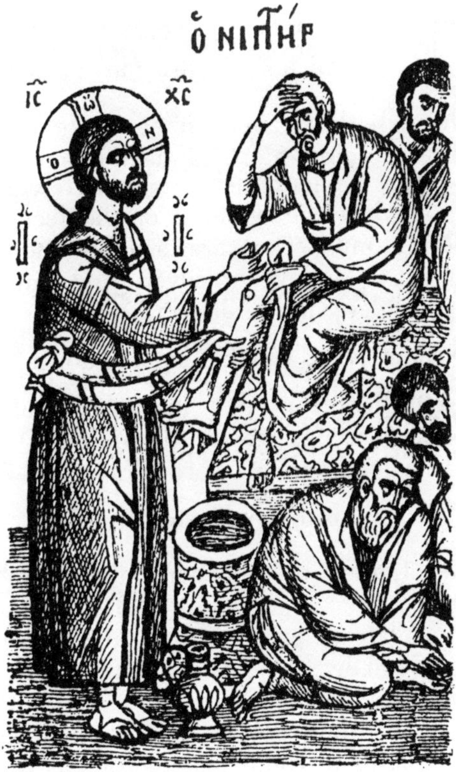
Ο ΝΙΠΤΗΡ
IC XC
Ο ΩΝ

ON THE FOLLOWING DAY

After the usual Morning Prayers, say:

Holy God. All-holy Trinity. Our Father.

Through the prayers of our holy Fathers, Lord Jesus Christ our God, have mercy on us. Amen.

Lord, have mercy (12). Glory; both now.

O come, let us worship and fall down before our King and God.
O come, let us worship and fall down before Christ, our King and God.
O come, let us worship and fall down before Him, Christ the King and our God.

PSALM 22

THE Lord is my shepherd, and I shall not want.
In a place of green pasture, there hath He made me to dwell; beside the water of rest hath He nurtured me.
He hath converted my soul, He hath led me on the paths of righteousness for His Name's sake.
For though I should walk in the midst of the shadow of death, I will fear no evil, for Thou

art with me; Thy rod and Thy staff, they have comforted me.

Thou hast prepared a table before me in the presence of them that afflict me.

Thou hast anointed my head with oil, and Thy cup which filleth me, how excellent it is!

And Thy mercy shall pursue me all the days of my life, and I will dwell in the house of the Lord unto length of days.

PSALM 23

THE earth is the Lord's, and the fulness thereof, the world, and all that dwell therein.

He hath founded it upon the seas, and upon the rivers hath He prepared it.

Who shall ascend into the mountain of the Lord? Or who shall stand in His holy place?

He that is innocent in hands and pure in heart, who hath not received his soul in vain, and hath not sworn deceitfully to his neighbour.

Such a one shall receive a blessing from the Lord, and mercy from God his Saviour.

This is the generation of them that seek the Lord, of them that seek the face of the God of Jacob.

Lift up your gates, O ye princes; and be ye lifted up, ye everlasting gates, and the King of Glory shall enter in.

Who is this King of Glory? The Lord strong and mighty, the Lord, mighty in war.

Lift up your gates, O ye princes; and be ye lifted up, ye everlasting gates, and the King of Glory shall enter in.

Who is this King of Glory? The Lord of hosts, He is the King of Glory.

PSALM 115

I BELIEVED, wherefore I spake; I was humbled exceedingly.

As for me, I said in mine ecstasy: Every man is a liar.

What shall I render unto the Lord for all that He hath rendered unto me?

I will take the cup of salvation, and I will call upon the Name of the Lord.

My vows unto the Lord will I pay in the presence of all His people.

Precious in the sight of the Lord is the death of His saints.

O Lord, I am Thy servant; I am Thy servant and the son of Thy handmaid. Thou hast broken my bonds asunder.

I will sacrifice a sacrifice of praise unto Thee, and I will call upon the Name of the Lord.

My vows unto the Lord will I pay in the presence of all His people, in the courts of the house of the Lord, in the midst of thee, O Jerusalem.

Then:

Glory to the Father, and to the Son, and to the Holy Spirit; both now and ever, and unto the ages of ages. Amen.

Alleluia, alleluia, alleluia: Glory to Thee, O God. (*3*)

Lord, have mercy. (*3*)

And the following Troparia:
Plagal of Fourth Tone

OVERLOOK mine iniquities, O Lord Who wast born of a Virgin, and purify my heart, and make it a temple for Thine immaculate Body and Blood. Cast me not away from Thy presence as one despised, O Thou Who hast immeasurably great mercy.

Glory.

HOW can I, the unworthy one, shamelessly dare to partake of Thy holy Gifts? For should I dare to approach Thee with those who are worthy, my vesture doth betray me, for it befitteth not the Supper, and I shall bring condemnation upon my sin-laden soul. Cleanse, O Lord, the defilement of my soul, and save me, since Thou art the Friend of man.

Both now.

GREAT are the multitudes of mine offences, O Theotokos; to thee have I fled, O pure one, and implore salvation. Visit mine ailing soul, and intercede with thy Son and our God that He may grant me forgiveness for the grievous deeds which I have committed, O only blessed one.

On Holy and Great Thursday, the following is said:

WHEN the glorious disciples were enlightened at the washing of the feet, then Judas the ungodly one was stricken and darkened with the love of silver. And unto the lawless judges did he deliver Thee, the righteous Judge. O thou lover of money, behold thou him who for the sake thereof did hang himself; flee from that insatiable soul that dared such things against the Master. O Thou Who art good unto all, Lord, glory be to Thee.

Then: **Lord, have mercy** (40). *As many prostrations as desired; then, straightway, the following supplicatory prayers:*

DIDACTIC VERSES
ON HOW ONE MUST APPROACH
THE IMMACULATE MYSTERIES

When thou, O man, art about to eat the Master's Body,
Draw nigh with fear, lest thou be seared; It is Fire.

And as thou drinkest the divine Blood unto
    communion,
First reconcile thyself with them that grieve
    thee,
Then, with daring, venture to eat the Mystic
    Food.

OTHER SIMILAR VERSES

Before partaking of the dread Sacrifice
Of the life-creating Body of the Master,
On this wise pray with trembling:

THE FIRST PRAYER,
OF SAINT BASIL THE GREAT

O MASTER, Lord Jesus Christ our God, the
Source of life and immortality, Who art
the Maker of all creation, both visible and invisible, the co-eternal and co-beginningless Son
of the beginningless Father, Who in the abundance of Thy goodness wast in the last days
clothed in flesh, wast crucified and buried for
us, the ungrateful and thankless ones, and by
Thine own Blood didst refashion our nature
which had been corrupted by sin: do Thou
Thyself, O immortal King, accept the repentance even of me, a sinner, and incline Thine
ear to me and hear my words. For I have
sinned, O Lord, I have sinned against Heaven
and before Thee, and I am not worthy to gaze

upon the height of Thy glory; for I have provoked Thy goodness by transgressing Thy commandments and by not obeying Thine ordinances. But Thou, O Lord, Who art forbearing, long-suffering, and plenteous in mercy, hast not given me up to perish in mine iniquities, most surely awaiting my conversion. For Thou, O Friend of man, hast said through Thy Prophet that Thou dost not desire with desire the death of the sinner, but that he should return and live. For Thou dost not will, O Master, that the work of Thy hands should perish, neither art Thou well-pleased in the perdition of men, but Thou desirest that all should be saved and come to the knowledge of the truth. Wherefore, though I am unworthy of both Heaven and earth, and even of this transient life, since I have wholly subjected myself to sin and am a slave to pleasures and have defaced Thine image, yet being Thy work and creation, I, the wretched one, do not despair of my salvation; but emboldened by Thine immeasurable compassion, I draw nigh. Wherefore, receive even me, O Christ, Thou Friend of man, as Thou didst the harlot, the thief, the publican, and the prodigal; and take away the heavy burden of my sins, O Thou that takest away the sin of the world, Who healest men's infirmities, Who callest to Thyself them that labour and are heavy laden and givest them rest, Who camest not to call the righteous, but sinners to repentance. And cleanse me of all defilement of flesh and spirit. Teach me to attain holiness in the fear of Thee, that, with the witness of my conscience pure, I may receive the portion of Thy holy Gifts and be united with Thy holy Body and Blood, and have Thee dwelling and abiding in me with the Father and Thy Holy Spirit. Yea, O Lord Jesus Christ, my God, let not the communion of Thine immaculate and life-creating Mysteries be to me for judgment, nor may I become infirm in soul and body by partaking of Them unworthily; but grant me till my last breath to receive without condemnation the portion of Thy holy Gifts, for communion with the Holy Spirit, as a provision for life everlasting, and for an acceptable defence at Thy dread tribunal, that even I, with all Thine elect, may become a partaker of Thine undefiled good things, which Thou hast prepared for them that love Thee, O Lord, in whom Thou art glorified unto the ages. Amen.

THE SECOND PRAYER,
OF SAINT BASIL THE GREAT

I KNOW, O Lord, that I partake of Thine immaculate Body and precious Blood unworthily, and that I am guilty, and eat and drink judgment to myself, not discerning the

Body and Blood of Thee, my Christ and God.
But, trusting in Thy compassions, I take courage and approach Thee, Who didst say: He that
eateth My Flesh and drinketh My Blood abideth in Me, and I in him. Wherefore, have compassion, O Lord, and make not an example of
me, the sinner, but deal with me according to
Thy mercy; and let these holy Gifts be unto my
healing, and purification, and enlightenment,
and protection, and salvation, and sanctification
of both soul and body, unto the averting of
every phantasy and evil deed and diabolical
operation working noetically in my members;
unto confidence and love toward Thee, unto
amendment of life and stability, unto an increase of virtue and perfection, unto fulfilment
of the commandments, unto communion with
the Holy Spirit, as a provision for life everlasting, and as an acceptable defence at Thy dread
tribunal, not unto judgment, nor unto condemnation.

THE THIRD PRAYER,
OF SAINT JOHN CHRYSOSTOM

O LORD my God, I know that I am not
worthy, nor sufficient, that Thou
shouldest come under the roof of the house of
my soul, for all is desolate and fallen, and Thou
hast not in me a place worthy to lay Thy head.
But even as from on high Thou didst humble

Thyself for our sake, so now conform Thyself to my lowliness. And even as Thou didst deign to lie in a cave and in a manger of irrational beasts, so also deign to lie in the manger of mine irrational soul and to enter my defiled body. And even as Thou didst not disdain to enter and dine with sinners in the house of Simon the leper, so consent also to enter the house of my lowly soul which is leprous and sinful. And even as Thou didst not reject the woman, who was a harlot and a sinner like me, when she approached and touched Thee, so also be compassionate with me, the sinner, as I approach and touch Thee. And as Thou didst not abhor her defiled and polluted mouth which kissed Thee, neither do Thou abhor my mouth, yet more defiled and polluted than hers, nor my lips which are loathsome, impure, and unholy, nor my tongue, yet more unclean. But let the live coal of Thine all-holy Body and Thy precious Blood be unto sanctification and enlightenment and strengthening of my humble soul and body, unto alleviation of the burden of my many offences, unto defence against every operation of the devil, unto the averting and hindering of my vile and wicked habits, unto the mortification of the passions, unto the accomplishment of Thy commandments, unto the increase of Thy divine grace, and unto the attainment of Thy Kingdom. For it is not as one presumptuous that I draw nigh to Thee, O Christ my God, but as one taking courage in Thine ineffable goodness, and that I may not, by long abstaining from Thy Communion, become a prey to the noetic wolf. Wherefore, I pray Thee Who alone art holy, O Master, sanctify my soul and body, my mind and heart, my reins and bowels, and wholly renew me. Root the fear of Thee in my members, and make Thy sanctification indelible within me. And be Thou my helper and defender, guide my life in peace, and make me worthy to stand at Thy right hand with Thy Saints, by the prayers and intercessions of Thine all-immaculate Mother, of Thine immaterial ministers and immaculate powers, and of all the Saints who, from ages past, have been well-pleasing unto Thee. Amen.

THE FOURTH PRAYER, OF SAINT JOHN CHRYSOSTOM

I AM not sufficient, O Master and Lord, that Thou shouldest enter under the roof of my soul; but since Thou, as the Friend of man, dost will to dwell in me, with trust I draw nigh. Thou commandest; I will open wide the gates which Thou alone hast fashioned, that Thou mayest enter, in Thy wonted love for man, that Thou mayest enter and enlighten my darkened thought. I believe that Thou wilt do this, for

Thou didst not shun the harlot who approached Thee with tears, nor didst Thou reject the publican who repented, nor didst Thou drive away the thief who acknowledged Thy Kingdom, nor didst Thou abandon the repentant persecutor as he was; but all who had been brought to Thee by repentance hast Thou established in the choir of Thy friends, O Thou Who alone art blessed, always, now and unto endless ages. Amen.

THE FIFTH PRAYER,
OF SAINT JOHN CHRYSOSTOM

O LORD Jesus Christ my God, loose, remit, forgive, and pardon the failings, faults, and offences which I, Thy sinful, unprofitable, and unworthy servant, have committed from my youth, up to the present day and hour, whether in knowledge or in ignorance, whether in words or deeds or thoughts, or reasonings and pursuits, or in any of my senses. And by the intercession of her that conceived Thee without seed, the immaculate and ever-virgin Mary, Thy Mother, mine only hope that putteth not to shame, my defence and salvation, do Thou count me worthy without condemnation to partake of Thine immaculate, immortal, life-creating, and dread Mysteries, unto forgiveness of sins and life everlasting, unto sanctification and enlightenment and strength and healing and health of both soul and body, and unto the blotting out and utter destruction of mine evil reasonings and thoughts and predispositions and nocturnal phantasies of the dark and evil spirits. For Thine is the kingdom, and the power, and the glory, and the honour, and the worship, with the Father and the Holy Spirit, now and ever, and unto the ages of ages. Amen.

THE SIXTH PRAYER, OF SAINT JOHN THE DAMASCENE

O MASTER, Lord Jesus Christ our God, Who alone hast authority to forgive men their sins: since Thou art good and the Friend of man, overlook all mine offences, whether committed in knowledge or in ignorance, and account me worthy to receive without condemnation Thy divine, glorious, immaculate, and life-creating Mysteries, not unto punishment, nor unto an increase of sins, but unto purification and sanctification and as an earnest of the life and kingdom to come, as a rampart and help, and for the overturning of adversaries, and for the blotting out of my many transgressions. For Thou art a God of mercy and compassions and love for man, and to Thee do we send up glory, with the Father and the Holy Spirit, now and ever, and unto the ages of ages. Amen.

THE SEVENTH PRAYER,
OF SAINT SYMEON THE NEW THEOLOGIAN

FROM lips tainted and defiled,
From a heart unclean and loathsome,
From a tongue befouled and filthy,
From a soul bestained and soiled,
O my Christ, receive my pleading.
Yea, disdain me not, nor shun me,
Nor my words, nor yet my manner,
Nor my shamelessness and boldness.
But with freedom let me tell Thee,
O my Christ, what I desire;
Rather, do Thou now instruct me
What I need to do and utter.
I have sinned more than the harlot
Who, on learning of Thy lodging,
Went and purchased myrrh most precious,
And with boldness she approached Thee,
To anoint Thy feet and lave them,
O my Christ, my God and Master.
Even as Thou didst not shun her
When she came with heartfelt fervour,
Thus, O Word, do not disdain me.
Nay, but rather do Thou grant me
To embrace Thy feet and kiss them,
And with streams of tears to wash them,
As with precious myrrh most costly,
With great boldness to anoint them.
Wash me with my tears, and thereby

Cleanse me, Word of God, and lave me.
Grant remission of my failings,
And bestow on me forgiveness.
All mine evil deeds Thou knowest,
And my wounds Thou knowest also,
And my bruises Thou beholdest.
But my faith Thou knowest likewise,
And mine eagerness Thou seest,
And my groans Thou hearest also.
There doth not escape Thy notice
Even one tear, O Redeemer,
Nor a fraction of a teardrop,
O my Lord God and Creator.
Yea, Thine eyes did see my being
While as yet it was unfashioned.
In Thy Book all thoughts and actions,
Even those not yet enacted,
Are inscribed for Thee already.
See my lowliness and toil!
Lo, the greatness of my suffering!
And, O God of all, forgive me
All the sins I have committed.
So that with a cleansed and pure heart,
And a mind with fear atremble,
And a soul contrite and lowly,
I may draw nigh to partake of
Thine all-pure and spotless Myst'ries,
Whereby all who eat and drink Thee
With a heart sincere and guileless
Are both deified and quickened.

For Thou sayest, O my Master:
He that eateth of My Flesh and
That doth drink of My Blood also
Doth abide in Me most truly,
And in him am I found also.
Wholly true is this word spoken
By my Lord and God and Master;
For whoever doth partake of
These divine and hallowed graces
Which impart deification
Is alone, in truth, no longer,
But is with Thee, Christ, Thou True Light
Of the Hallowed, Triple Daystar,
Which illumineth the whole world.
Lest, then, I remain alone now
And apart from Thee, Lifegiver,
O my Breath, my Life, my Gladness,
The entire world's Salvation,
For this cause do I approach Thee
With a soul contrite and tearful.
O Thou Ransom of my failings,
I entreat Thee to receive me,
So that I may now partake of
Thy life-giving, blameless Myst'ries,
And not suffer condemnation;
That, as Thou didst say, Thou mightest
Dwell with me, who am thrice-wretched;
Lest that foul deceiver find me
All bereft of Thy divine grace,
And most guilefully seduce me,

And with scheming cunning lure me
From Thy words which make me Godlike.
Wherefore, I fall down before Thee,
And cry out to Thee with fervour:
As Thou didst receive and welcome
Both the prodigal and harlot
Who drew nigh to Thee, so likewise,
O Most Merciful, receive me,
The great profligate and sinner,
The most prodigal and vile one,
As I dare now to approach Thee
With a soul contrite and humbled.
Saviour, well I know that no one
Hath sinned as have I against Thee,
Nor hath wrought the deeds which I have.
Yet again, I know this also:
Neither greatness of transgressions,
Nor enormity in sinning,
Can surpass my God and Saviour's
Great long-suffering and mercy
And exceeding love for mankind.
For with the oil of compassion
Thou dost cleanse and render shining
All those who repent with fervour;
And Thou makest them partakers
Of Thy light in all abundance,
And true sharers of Thy Godhood.
And—O marvel for the Angels
And for human understanding!—
Thou hast converse with them often

As with friends most true and trusted.
These things now do give me daring,
These things give me wings, O Christ God;
Trusting, then, in the abundance
Of Thy benefactions toward us,
With rejoicing, yet with trembling,
I partake now of the Fire.
Though but grass—O awesome wonder!—
Yet bedewed am I past telling,
Like that bush of old on Sinai
Which was unconsumed, though burning.
Wherefore, with a mind most thankful,
And a heart most thankful also,
Thankful also in the members
Of my soul and of my body,
I adore and magnify Thee,
O my God, and glorify Thee,
As One verily most blessed,
Now and ever, to all ages.

THE EIGHTH PRAYER,
OF SAINT SYMEON METAPHRASTES

O LORD, Who alone art pure and incorrupt, Who through the ineffable compassion of Thy love for man didst assume our whole substance from the pure and virginal blood of her that, in a manner surpassing nature, conceived Thee by the coming of the Divine Spirit and by the good will of the Everlasting Father; O Christ Jesus, the Wisdom, Peace, and Power of God; O Thou Who, in that nature taken upon Thyself, didst accept Thy life-creating and saving Passion, the Cross, the nails, the spear, and death: do Thou mortify all the soul-corrupting passions of my body. Thou Who by Thy burial didst despoil the dominions of Hades: do Thou bury with good thoughts mine evil schemes and dispel the spirits of wickedness. Thou Who by Thy life-creating Resurrection on the third day didst raise up our fallen first parent: raise me up who have slipped down into sin, and set before me the ways of repentance. Thou Who by Thy glorious Ascension didst deify the flesh that Thou hadst taken upon Thyself and didst honour it by Thy session at the right hand of the Father: by my partaking of Thy holy Mysteries make me worthy of the portion of the saved at Thy right hand. Thou Who by the coming of the Comforter, Thy Spirit, didst make Thy sacred Disciples precious vessels: show me forth also as a receptacle of His coming. Thou Who art to come again to judge the world in righteousness: be it Thy good will that I also meet Thee in the clouds, O my Creator and Fashioner, with all Thy Saints, that without end I may glorify and hymn Thee, with Thy Father which is without beginning, and Thine All-holy and good and life-creating Spirit, now and ever, and unto the ages of ages. Amen.

THE NINTH PRAYER,
OF SAINT JOHN THE DAMASCENE

I STAND before the doors of Thy temple, yet I do not put away my grievous thoughts. But do Thou, O Christ God, Who didst justify the publican, and have mercy on the Canaanitish woman, and open the gates of Paradise to the thief, open unto me the bowels of Thy love for man; and as I approach and touch Thee, receive me like the woman with an issue of blood and like the harlot. For the one, by touching the hem of Thy garment received healing readily, and the other, by clasping Thine immaculate feet obtained release from her sins. And I, deplorable though I be, dare to receive Thy whole Body; may I not be consumed, but receive me even as these. And do Thou enlighten the senses of my soul, and burn up the indictments of my sins, by the intercessions of her that seedlessly bare Thee, and of the heavenly hosts, for blessed art Thou unto the ages of ages. Amen.

THE TENTH PRAYER,
OF SAINT JOHN CHRYSOSTOM

I BELIEVE, O Lord, and I confess that Thou art truly the Christ, the Son of the Living God, Who camest into the world to save sinners, of whom I am chief. Furthermore, I believe that This is indeed Thine immaculate

Body, and that This is indeed Thy precious Blood. Wherefore, I pray Thee: Have mercy on me and forgive me my transgressions, voluntary and involuntary, in word and deed, in knowledge and in ignorance. And vouchsafe that, uncondemned, I may partake of Thine immaculate Mysteries unto the remission of sins and unto life everlasting. Amen.

When thou art about to communicate, say the following verses of Saint Symeon Metaphrastes:

Behold, I approach Divine Communion;
O Maker, burn me not as I partake,
For Fire art Thou which burneth the unworthy.
But purify Thou me of every stain.

Then the Troparion:

OF Thy Mystic Supper, O Son of God, receive me today as a communicant; for I will not speak of the Mystery to Thine enemies; nor will I give Thee a kiss as did Judas; but like the thief do I confess Thee: Remember me, O Lord, in Thy Kingdom.

And also these verses:

Tremble, O man, as thou beholdest the deifying Blood,
For it is a burning coal consuming the unworthy.

The Body of God both deifieth and nourisheth
me;
It deifieth the spirit and wondrously nourisheth
the mind.

And these Troparia:

THOU hast smitten me with yearning, O
Christ, and by Thy divine love hast Thou
changed me. But with Thine immaterial fire,
consume my sins and count me worthy to be
filled with delight in Thee, that leaping for joy,
O Good One, I may magnify Thy two comings.

INTO the splendour of Thy Saints how shall
I, the unworthy one, enter? For should I dare
to enter the bridal chamber, my vesture doth
betray me, for it is not a wedding garment; and
as one bound, I shall be cast out by the Angels.
Cleanse, O Lord, the defilement of my soul,
and save me, since Thou art the Friend of man.

And this prayer:

O MAN-BEFRIENDING Master, Lord Jesus
my God, let not these holy Gifts be unto
me for judgment through mine unworthiness,
but for the purification and sanctification of
both soul and body, and as an earnest of the
life and the kingdom to come. For it is good for
me to cleave unto God and to place in the Lord
the hope of my salvation.

And again:

OF Thy Mystic Supper, O Son of God, receive me today as a communicant; for I will not speak of the Mystery to Thine enemies; nor will I give Thee a kiss as did Judas; but like the thief do I confess Thee: Remember me, O Lord, in Thy Kingdom. Remember me, O Master, in Thy Kingdom. Remember me, O Holy One, in Thy Kingdom.

Straightway upon receiving the Body and Blood of the Saviour, say the following quietly to thyself:

BEHOLD, This hath touched thy lips, and will take away thine iniquities, and will purge thy sins. (*Esaias 6:7*)

THANKSGIVING
AFTER HOLY COMMUNION

And having attained the good Communion
Of the life-creating and mystic Gifts,
Straightway give praise and great thanksgiving,
And fervently, from thy soul, cry unto God:

> Glory to Thee, O God;
> Glory to Thee, O God;
> Glory to Thee, O God.

And straightway the following prayers:

ANONYMOUS

I THANK Thee, O Lord my God, that Thou
hast not rejected me, the sinner, but hast
deemed me worthy to be a communicant of
Thy holy Mysteries. I thank Thee that Thou
hast deemed me worthy, unworthy as I am, to
partake of Thine immaculate and heavenly
Gifts. But, O man-befriending Master, Who
didst die for us and rise again and didst grant

373

us these Thy dread and life-creating Mysteries for the benefit and sanctification of our souls and bodies, grant also that these may be unto me for the healing of both soul and body, for the averting of everything hostile, for the enlightenment of the eyes of my heart, for the peace of the powers of my soul, for love unfeigned, for faith unashamed, for the plenitude of wisdom, for the keeping of Thy commandments, for an increase of Thy divine grace, and for the attainment of Thy Kingdom; that being kept by them in Thy holiness I may ever remember Thy grace, and never live for myself, but for Thee, our Master and Benefactor. And thus, when from this life I have passed in the hope of life eternal, may I attain to everlasting rest where the sound is unceasing of them that keep festival, and unending the delight of them that behold the ineffable beauty of Thy countenance. For Thou art the true desire and the unutterable gladness of them that love Thee, O Christ our God, and all creation praiseth Thee unto the ages. Amen.

A PRAYER OF
SAINT BASIL THE GREAT

O MASTER, Christ God, King of the ages and Creator of all, I thank Thee for all the good things Thou hast bestowed upon me and for the participation in Thine immaculate and life-creating Mysteries. I pray Thee, therefore, O Good One, Thou Friend of man, guard me under Thy protection and in the shadow of Thy wings; and grant that with a pure conscience till my last breath I may worthily partake of Thy holy Gifts unto forgiveness of sins and life everlasting. For Thou art the Bread of life, the Well-spring of holiness, and the Giver of all that is good; and to Thee we send up glory, with the Father and the Holy Spirit, now and ever, and unto the ages of ages. Amen.

A PRAYER OF
SAINT SYMEON METAPHRASTES

THOU Who givest me willingly as nourishment Thy Flesh,
Thou Who art fire, and dost consume the unworthy,
Scorch me not, O my Maker,
But rather pass through me for the right ordering of my members,
Into all my joints, my reins, and my heart.
Burn up the thorns of all mine offences.
Purify my soul; sanctify my mind;
Make firm my knees and bones;
Enlighten the simple unity of my five senses.
Nail down the whole of me with Thy fear.
Ever shelter, guard, and keep me
From every soul-corrupting deed and word.
Purify, and cleanse, and order me aright;

Make me comely, give me understanding, and
    enlighten me.
Show me forth as the habitation of the Spirit
    only,
And no longer as a habitation of sin,
That as Thine abode from the entrance in of
    Thy Communion
Every evil-doer and passion may flee from me
    like fire.
As intercessors I bring to Thee all the sanc-
    tified:
The ranks of the incorporeal Powers,
Thy Forerunner, the wise Apostles,
And further, Thy pure and spotless Mother.
The prayers of these receive, O my compas-
    sionate Christ,
And make of me who worship Thee a child of
    light.
For Thou alone art our sanctification, O Good
    One,
And the illumination of our souls;
And to Thee, as to our God and Master, we,
    each day,
As is fitting, all send up glory.

ANONYMOUS

MAY Thy holy Body, O Lord Jesus Christ
our God, be unto me for eternal life, and
Thy precious Blood for the forgiveness of sins.
And may this Eucharist be unto me for joy,

health, and gladness. And in Thy dread second coming, make me, the sinner, worthy to stand at the right hand of Thy glory, by the intercessions of Thine all-immaculate Mother and of all Thy Saints. Amen.

TO THE MOST HOLY THEOTOKOS

O ALL-HOLY Lady Theotokos, the light of my darkened soul, my hope and protection, my refuge and consolation, and my joy, I thank thee that thou hast deemed me, the unworthy one, worthy to be a communicant of the immaculate Body and the precious Blood of thy Son. But do thou who gavest birth to the true Light, enlighten the noetic eyes of my heart. O thou who didst conceive the Source of immortality, give life to me who am dead in sin. O thou who art the compassionately loving Mother of the merciful God, have mercy on me and give me compunction and contrition of heart, humility in my reasonings, and the recall of my thoughts from their captivity. And deem me worthy, till my last breath, to receive without condemnation the sanctification of the immaculate Mysteries unto healing of both soul and body. And grant me tears of repentance and confession, that I may hymn and glorify thee all the days of my life.

For blessed and glorified art thou
unto the ages (3). Amen.

Then:

Now lettest Thou Thy servant depart in peace, O Master, according to Thy word, for mine eyes have seen Thy salvation, which Thou hast prepared before the face of all peoples: a light of revelation for the nations, and the glory of Thy people Israel.

And straightway:

Holy God. All-holy Trinity. Our Father.

Then continue:

(But note that when these prayers are read aloud in church, the order beginning on page 381 is used in place of the following.)

If the Divine Liturgy of Saint John Chrysostom was celebrated, say:

DISMISSAL HYMN

Grace shining forth from thy mouth like a beacon hath illumined the universe, and disclosed to the world treasures of uncovetousness, and shown us the heights of humility; but whilst instructing us by thy words, O Father John Chrysostom, intercede with the Word, Christ our God, to save our souls.

Glory.

KONTAKION

From the Heavens hast thou received divine grace, and by thy lips thou dost teach all to worship the One God in Trinity, O John Chrysostom, all-blessed righteous one. Rightly do we acclaim thee, for thou art a teacher revealing things divine.

Both now.

BY the intercession, O Lord, of all the Saints and the Theotokos, do Thou grant us Thy peace, and have mercy on us, since Thou alone art compassionate.

But if the Divine Liturgy of Saint Basil the Great was celebrated, say:

DISMISSAL HYMN

THY sound hath gone forth into all the earth, which hath received thy word. Thereby thou hast divinely taught the Faith; thou hast made manifest the nature of all things that be; thou hast adorned the ways of man. O namesake of the royal priesthood, our righteous Father Basil, intercede with Christ God that our souls be saved.

Glory.
KONTAKION

FOR the Church art thou in truth a firm foundation, granting an inviolate lordship unto all mortal men and sealing it with what thou hast taught, O righteous Basil, revealer of heavenly things.

Both now.

B Y the intercession, O Lord, of all the Saints
and the Theotokos, do Thou grant us Thy
peace, and have mercy on us, since Thou alone
art compassionate.

*Or, if the Liturgy of the Presanctified Gifts was cele-
brated, say:*

DISMISSAL HYMN OF SAINT GREGORY
THE GREAT, POPE OF ROME

A S one endowed with discretion of speech,
thou didst prove to be a most excellent
dispenser of the word of God, O hierarch Gregory; for by thy life thou didst set the virtues
before us, and thou dost shine forth with the
brilliance of holiness. O righteous Father, do
thou entreat Christ God that we be granted
great mercy.

Glory.
KONTAKION

T O thee, who art the Church's tuneful harp
inspired of God, thou tongue of wisdom
who wast verily possessed of God, unto thee,
as it is meet, we now offer praises; for thou
truly hadst the zeal of the Apostles' choir and
didst follow in their footsteps as their worthy
heir; and to thee we say: Rejoice, divine Father
Gregory.

Both now.

By the intercession, O Lord, of all the Saints and the Theotokos, do Thou grant us Thy peace, and have mercy on us, since Thou alone art compassionate.

And straightway:

Lord, have mercy (12). Glory; both now.

More honourable than the Cherubim, and beyond compare more glorious than the Seraphim, thee who without corruption gavest birth to God the Word, the very Theotokos, thee do we magnify.

Through the prayers of our holy Fathers, Lord Jesus Christ our God, have mercy on us. Amen.

When the Prayers of Thanksgiving after Holy Communion are read aloud in church, after the **Our Father**:

First, if it be the Lord's Day, the Resurrection Dismissal Hymn of the tone of the week.

Then the Dismissal Hymn of the current Feast of the Master or of the Mother of God, if one is being celebrated.

Then the Dismissal Hymn of the Saint to whom the temple is dedicated. (Note that if the temple is named in honour of a Feast of the Master or of the Theotokos, its Dismissal Hymn is omitted when a major feast is celebrated.)

Then the Dismissal Hymn(s) of the Saint(s) of the day.

Then the Dismissal Hymn of the Saint whose Divine Liturgy was celebrated (see pages 378–380).

Then, if it be the Lord's Day, the Resurrection Kontakion of the tone of the week.

Then the Kontakion of the current Feast of the Master or of the Mother of God, if one is being celebrated.

Then the Kontakion of the Saint to whom the temple is dedicated. (Note here also that if the temple is named in honour of a Feast of the Master or of the Theotokos, its Kontakion is omitted when a major feast is celebrated.)

Then the Kontakion (Kontakia) of the Saint(s) of the day.

Then the Kontakion of the Saint whose Divine Liturgy was celebrated (see pages 378–380).

And straightway:

Lord, have mercy (12). Glory; both now.

MORE honourable than the Cherubim, and beyond compare more glorious than the Seraphim, thee who without corruption gavest birth to God the Word, the very Theotokos, thee do we magnify.

In the Name of the Lord, Father, bless.

The priest: God be gracious unto us and bless

us, and cause His face to shine upon us and have mercy on us.

The reader: **Amen.** *And he readeth the following Megalynarion:*

(But note that on Feasts of the Master and of the Theotokos, instead of the following Megalynarion, the Megalynarion of the feast—that is, the hymn which replaceth **It is truly meet to call thee blest** *in the Divine Liturgy—is read instead.)*

IN thee, O Full of Grace, all creation—both the company of Angels and the race of men—doth rejoice. O hallowed temple and spiritual paradise, boast of virgins: from thee God was incarnate, and became a child, He, our God, Who existed before the ages; for He made thy womb a throne, and He made thee more spacious than the heavens. In thee, O Full of Grace, all creation doth rejoice. Glory be to thee.

Then:

Glory to the Father, and to the Son, and to the Holy Spirit; both now and ever, and unto the ages of ages. Amen.

Lord, have mercy (3). Holy Father, bless.

The priest maketh the accustomed dismissal, and then saith:

Through the prayers of our holy Fathers, Lord Jesus Christ our God, have mercy on us.

The reader: **Amen.**

A PRAYER BOOK
FOR ORTHODOX CHRISTIANS

was typeset in Linotype Aldus by the Holy
Transfiguration Monastery and printed by
Friesens in Altona, Manitoba, in an edition
of five thousand copies on Glatfelter Offset,
an acid-free paper of proven durability.

GLORY BE TO GOD FOR ALL THINGS.
AMEN.